JEWELS
OF
FORMAL
LANGUAGE THEORY

BOOKS OF INTEREST

JEWELS
OF
FORMAL
LANGUAGE THEORY

ARTO SALOMAA

University of Turku
Turku, Finland

COMPUTER SCIENCE PRESS

Computer Science Press, Inc.
11 Taft Court.
Rockville, Maryland 20850

1 2 3 4 5 6   86 85 84 83 82 81

Library of Congress Cataloging in Publication Data

Salomaa, Arto.
    Jewels of formal language theory.

    Bibliography: p.
    Includes index.
    1. Formal languages. I. Title.
QA267.3.S25   511.3   80-24269
ISBN 0-914894-69-2

Cover design by Ruth Ramminger

To the memory of my father
J. E. Salomaa

Acknowledgements

I want to express my gratitude to the Academy of Finland for good working conditions during the writing of this book. It is difficult to list all persons who have in some way or other contributed to this book. I have benefited from discussions with or comments from W. Bucher, K. Culik II, J. Karhumäki, M. Linna, J. Mäenpää, H. Maurer, G. Rozenberg, K. Ruohonen, and D. Wood. The difficult task of typing the manuscript was performed most carefully by Elisa Söderblom. Finally, I want to thank Computer Science Press, and in particular Dana W. Lane and Brenda L. Newland, for excellent and timely editorial work with both the manuscript and proofs.

Arto Salomaa
November 1980

Preface

The need for a formal grammatical description of specific languages arises in various scientific disciplines. This makes formal language theory a really interdisciplinary area of science. Indeed, this fact is apparent also in the historical development of the area: while the oldest trends come from pure mathematics, the more recent ones originate from attempts to model natural languages, artificial languages of computer science, or even the development of filamentous organisms.

Formal language theory has been viewed as part of the mainstream of research, and it has also been considered to be only of minor importance—the judgment seems to vary according to time and geographic location of the judges. However, I would certainly agree with another Finn, Alfred Aho, who in a recent lecture referred to formal language theory as "the flower of computer science" where some other areas, such as complexity, programming languages, systems and compilers, can be seen as petals.

The purpose of this book is to present in a self-contained and compact form some elegant results from formal language theory. I have had two aims in mind: (i) to give an introduction of the theory for an uninitiated reader, and (ii) to include a considerable amount of material of current research interest. I hope that the book can be used as a text in a short course because of (i) and is also of interest to the researcher because of (ii). It is by no means claimed that this book contains *all* "jewels" of the theory, or that the results presented are always more beautiful than those omitted. It is even possible that some specialist will miss his or her favorite jewel. Because of our aim (i) and the fact that the book is self-contained and of a rather small size, it is not possible to present material from very diverse areas. The "common denominator" in this book is the notion of a morphism on a free monoid.

Although the book is self-contained and assumes no previous knowledge on the part of the reader, it definitely assumes some mathematical maturity. Because of our aim (ii), some of the results presented are rather difficult ones. And even in general one cannot expect a beautiful result to be trivial! A reader with some background in formal language theory will notice that, regarding the families in the basic Chomsky hierarchy, the family of context-sensitive languages is hardly mentioned. Indeed, it has been apparent for a long time that this family is not interesting from the point of view of applications. And I think that very few interesting theoretical results have been obtained for this family or its relation to the theory as a whole. The other families in the Chomsky hierarchy, as well as the family of DOL languages, are discussed rather extensively.

Contents

Chapter 1

REPETITIONS

1.1 WORDS AND LANGUAGES

Our first topic is repetitions of words. This is the oldest topic studied in formal language theory, going back to the work of Axel Thue at the beginning of this century. Thue's results have been rediscovered many times in various disguises. Before discussing the results themselves, we have to introduce some notions and terminology needed throughout this book.

An *alphabet* is a finite nonempty set. The elements of an alphabet Σ are called *letters* or *symbols*. A *word* over an alphabet Σ is a finite string consisting of zero or more letters of Σ, whereby the same letter may occur several times. The string consisting of zero letters is called the *empty word*, written λ. Thus, λ, 0, 1, 010, 1111 are words over the alphabet $\Sigma = \{0, 1\}$. The set of all words (resp. all nonempty words) over an alphabet Σ is denoted by Σ^* (resp. Σ^+). The set Σ^* is infinite for any Σ. Algebraically, Σ^* and Σ^+ are the free monoid and free semigroup generated by Σ.

The reader should keep in mind that the basic set Σ, its elements and strings of its elements could equally well be called a vocabulary, words and sentences, respectively. This would reflect an approach aiming at applications mainly in the field of natural languages. In this book, we stick to the standard mathematical terminology introduced above.

If x and y are words over an alphabet Σ, then so is their *catenation xy*. Catenation is an associative operation, and the empty word is an identity with respect to catenation: $x\lambda = \lambda x = x$ holds for all words x. For a word x and a natural number i, the notation x^i means the word obtained by catenating i copies of the word x. By definition, x^0 is the empty word λ.

The *length* of a word x, in symbols $|x|$, is the number of letters in x when each letter is counted as many times as it occurs. Again by definition, $|\lambda| = 0$. The length function possesses some of the formal properties of logarithm:

$$|xy| = |x| + |y|, \; |x^i| = i|x|,$$

for any words x and y and integers $i \geq 0$.

1

A word x is a *subword* of a word y if there are words x_1 and x_2 such that $y = x_1 x x_2$. Furthermore, if $x_1 = \lambda$ (resp. $x_2 = \lambda$), then x is called an *initial subword* or *prefix* of y (resp. a *final* subword or a *suffix* of y).

Subsets of Σ^* are referred to as (*formal*) *languages* over Σ. Thus,

$$L_1 = \{a, ba, aaba, b^5\} \quad \text{and} \quad L_2 = \{a^p \mid p \text{ prime}\}$$

are languages over the alphabet $\Sigma = \{a, b\}$, the former being finite and the latter infinite. A finite language can, at least in principle, be defined by listing all of its words. Such a procedure is not possible for infinite languages: some finitary specification other than simple listing is needed to define an infinite language. Formal language theory deals mainly with such finitary specifications of infinite languages. We shall meet some classes of them later on in this book.

The reader might find our terminology somewhat unusual: a language should consist of sentences rather than of words, as is the case in our terminology. However, as pointed out above, this is irrelevant and depends merely on the choice of the basic terminology, and anyone who feels strongly about it can rename the latter.

An operation of crucial importance in language theory is the operation of morphism. A mapping $h : \Sigma^* \to \Delta^*$, where Σ and Δ are alphabets, satisfying the condition

$$h(xy) = h(x)h(y), \text{ for all words } x \text{ and } y, \tag{1.1}$$

is called a *morphism*. For languages L over Σ we define

$$h(L) = \{h(w) \mid w \text{ is in } L\}.$$

(Thus, algebraically, a morphism of languages is a monoid morphism linearly extended to subsets of monoids.) Because of the condition (1.1), to define a morphism h, it suffices to list all the words $h(a)$, where a ranges over all the (finitely many) letters of Σ.

Triples $G = (\Sigma, h, w)$, where Σ is an alphabet, $h : \Sigma^* \to \Sigma^*$ is a morphism and w is a word over Σ, are referred to as *DOL systems*. A DOL system G defines the following sequence $S(G)$ of words over Σ:

$$w = h^0(w), h(w) = h^1(w), h(h(w)) = h^2(w), h^3(w), \ldots .$$

It also defines the following language

$$L(G) = \{h^i(w) \mid i \geq 0\}.$$

Thus, a DOL system constitutes a very simple finitary device for language definition. Languages defined by a DOL system are referred to as *DOL languages*. We shall discuss them later on in Chapter 5, and we will also explain the abbreviation "DOL."

An infinite sequence of elements of an alphabet Σ is called an ω-*word*. Thus, an ω-word can be identified with a mapping of the set of nonnegative integers into Σ. A very convenient way of defining some special ω-words is provided by DOL systems as follows. Consider a DOL system $G = (\Sigma, h, w)$ such that

$$h(w) = wx, \text{ where } x \in \Sigma^+, \tag{1.2}$$

that is, w is a proper prefix of $h(w)$, and furthermore, h is *nonerasing*: $h(a) \neq \lambda$ for every a in Σ. Then by (1.2)

$$h^2(w) = wxh(x), \; h^3(w) = wxh(x)h^2(x)$$

and, in general,

$$h^{i+1}(w) = h^i(w)h^i(x) \text{ for all } i \geq 0. \tag{1.3}$$

The equation (1.3) shows that, for any i, $h^i(w)$ is a proper prefix of $h^{i+1}(w)$. (Observe that $h^i(x) \neq \lambda$ because h is nonerasing.) Consequently, an ω-word α can be defined as the "limit" of the sequence $h^i(w)$, $i = 0, 1, 2, \ldots$. More explicitly, α is the ω-word whose prefix of length $|h^i(w)|$ equals $h^i(w)$, for all i. (The notions of a prefix and a subword are extended to concern ω-words in the natural fashion. A word x is a subword of an ω-word α if α can be written as $x_1x\alpha_1$, where x_1 is a word and α_1 is an ω-word. If moreover $x_1 = \lambda$, then x is a prefix of α.) The ω-word α obtained in this fashion is said to be *generated* by the DOL system G.

1.2 THUE'S PROBLEM

The problem deals with repetitions occurring in words and ω-words. A word or an ω-word over an alphabet Σ is termed *square-free* (resp. *cube-free*) if it contains no subword of the form x^2 (resp. x^3), where x is a nonempty word. A word or an ω-word is termed *strongly cube-free* if it contains no subword of the form x^2a, where x is a nonempty word and a is the first letter of x. Clearly, every square-free word or ω-word is also strongly cube-free, and every strongly cube-free word or ω-word is also cube-free.

Thue's problem consists of constructing square-free words, as long as possible, over a given alphabet Σ, and preferably square-free ω-words.

Whenever this is not possible, strongly cube-free words or ω-words should be constructed, again as long as possible. Applications of Thue's problem arise in a variety of quite different situations, some of which are mentioned in Exercises 6–9 below.

As an initial observation, it should be noted that Thue's problem becomes easier (in a sense made precise below) if the cardinality of the alphabet Σ increases. Intuitively, this provides more "leeway." In particular, if Σ consists of only one letter, then no word of length ≥ 3 is cube-free. If Σ consists of two letters, then only very short words can be square-free, as seen in the following lemma.

Lemma 1.1.   No word of length ≥ 4 over an alphabet Σ with cardinality 2 is square-free. Consequently, no ω-word over Σ is square-free.

Proof.   Let Σ consist of the letters a and b. The only square-free words of length 3 are

$$aba \quad \text{and} \quad bab \qquad\qquad (1.4)$$

because the other words of length 3

$$a^3, \, a^2b, \, ba^2, \, b^3, \, b^2a, \, ab^2$$

all contain either a^2 or b^2 as a subword. On the other hand, no matter in what way another letter is added to one of the words (1.4), the resulting word always contains one of the words a^2, b^2, $(ab)^2$, $(ba)^2$ as a subword and, consequently, is not square-free.   □

Let α be a word (resp. an ω-word) over an alphabet Σ. A word α' of the same length as α (resp. an ω-word α') is called an *interpretation* of α if the following condition is satisfied: whenever the ith symbol (counted from the beginning) differs from the jth symbol in α, then also in α' the ith symbol differs from the jth symbol. Thus, both $a_1a_2a_3b_1a_4b_2$ and $a_1a_2a_1a_3a_1a_3$ are interpretations of the word a^3bab, whereas $a_1a_2a_3a_4a_5a_1$ is not an interpretation of a^3bab, because the first and last letter in a^3bab are different. Apart from a possible renaming of the letters, every interpretation of a word or ω-word α is obtained by providing, for each letter a in α, every occurrence of a with some lower index, where only a finite number of indices may be used. Interpretations will be met also in Chapter 7 below.

Lemma 1.2.   If α (a word or an ω-word) is square-free, strongly cube-free or cube-free, then so is every interpretation α' of α.

Proof. The assertion follows directly by the definition of an interpretation. For instance, if α' has a subword of the form x^2, then the subword occurring in the same position in α must be of the form y^2. □

Lemma 1.2 shows that if α is a square-free, (resp. strongly cube-free, cube-free) ω-word strictly over an alphabet Σ (meaning that all letters of Σ actually occur in α) and Σ_1 is an alphabet of cardinality greater than that of Σ, then a square-free (resp. strongly cube-free, cube-free) ω-word strictly over Σ_1 can be constructed from α.

Returning to Thue's problem, it is obvious that if we are able to construct a square-free (resp. strongly cube-free) ω-word over an alphabet Σ, then we can also construct arbitrarily long square-free (resp. strongly cube-free) words over Σ. (The converse implication is not so obvious; however, it turns out to be true as we shall see below.) Consequently, in view of Lemma 1.1, the best results we can hope for are the solutions to the following two problems.

 (i) Construct a strongly cube-free ω-word over an alphabet with cardinality 2. (*Strong cube-freeness problem.*)
(ii) Construct a square-free ω-word over an alphabet with cardinality 3. (*Square-freeness problem.*)

By Lemma 1.2, solutions to problems (i) and (ii) imply that we can construct strongly cube-free (resp. square-free) ω-words, as well as arbitrarily long words with this property, over any alphabet with cardinality ≥ 2 (resp. ≥ 3).

We shall now give a solution to problems (i) and (ii). Readers who are able to find a solution themselves might have been forerunners of formal language theory like Axel Thue.

1.3 SOLUTION TO THE STRONG CUBE-FREENESS PROBLEM

Consider a DOL system $G = (\{a, b\}, h, a)$, where the morphism h is defined by

$$h(a) = ab, h(b) = ba.$$

Then the first few words in the sequence $S(G)$ are

$$a, ab, abba, abba\ baab, abba\ baab\ baab\ abba, \ldots .$$

In general, for any $i \geq 1$, the $(i + 1)$st word w_{i+1} in the sequence $S(G)$ satisfies

$$w_{i+1} = w_i w_i', \qquad\qquad (1.5)$$

where we denote by x' the word obtained from the word x by interchanging a and b.

We prove (1.5) inductively, observing first that it holds for $i = 1$. Assuming (1.5) for a fixed value i, we complete the inductive step as follows:

$$w_{i+2} = h(w_{i+1}) = h(w_i w_i') = h(w_i)h(w_i')$$
$$= w_{i+1}h(w_i') = w_{i+1}w_{i+1}',$$

where the last equation follows because

$$h(x') = (h(x))'$$

holds for any word x, by the definition of h.

Denote now by α the ω-word generated by G. Our aim is to show that α is strongly cube-free. Observe that (1.5) provides a convenient way of writing down an arbitrarily long prefix of α. Following the grouping due to (1.5), we obtain

$$a \quad b \quad ba \quad baab \quad baababba \quad baababbaabbabaab \quad \ldots \quad (1.6)$$

Thus, (1.6) shows the beginning of α. The empty spaces are only used to indicate the position where a new w_i' has been added.

We need some properties of the ω-word α for the proof of the main result. It will be useful to consider α also in the form

$$\alpha = c_1 c_2 c_3 \ldots , \quad (1.7)$$

where each c_j equals either a or b.

Lemma 1.3. Neither a^3 nor b^3 occurs as a subword in α. Neither $ababa$ nor $babab$ occurs as a subword in α. Consequently, every subword x of α such that $|x| = 5$ contains either a^2 or b^2 as a subword.

Proof. Consider the first sentence. If either a^3 or b^3 occurs as a subword in α, then it occurs as a subword in some w_i. But this is impossible because $w_i = h(w_{i-1})$ and, consequently, w_i is obtained by catenating words ab and ba in some order.

Consider the second sentence. Assume that $ababa$ occurs as a subword of α, starting with the jth letter of α. Thus, in the notation of (1.7),

$$c_j c_{j+1} c_{j+2} c_{j+3} c_{j+4} = ababa. \tag{1.8}$$

We choose an i large enough such that

$$|w_i| \geq j + 4.$$

Thus, the occurrence (1.8) is already in w_i. We use again the relation $w_i = h(w_{i-1})$ and conclude that either a^3 or b^3 occurs as a subword in w_{i-1}, depending on whether j in (1.8) is odd or even. But this cannot happen because of the already established first sentence of our lemma. In the same way (or arguing by symmetry) we see that $babab$ does not occur as a subword of α.

Finally, the last sentence is a consequence of the second sentence because, apart from the words $ababa$ and $babab$, every word of length 5 over $\{a, b\}$ contains a^2 or b^2 as a subword. $\square$

Lemma 1.4. Assume that a^2 or b^2 occurs as a subword of α, starting with the jth letter of α. Then j is even.

Proof. We use the notation of (1.7), assuming that $c_j c_{j+1}$ equals either a^2 or b^2. We choose again an i large enough such that

$$|w_i| \geq j + 1,$$

and make use of the relation $w_i = h(w_{i-1})$. Because of this relation, j being odd implies that $c_j c_{j+1}$ equals either $h(a)$ or $h(b)$. Since neither one of the latter equals a^2 or b^2, we obtain the lemma. $\square$

We are now in the position to establish our main result.

Theorem 1.5. The ω-word α is strongly cube-free.

Proof. Arguing again indirectly, we assume that xxc, where c is the first letter of x, is a subword of α and, furthermore, no word yyd, where d is the first letter of y and $|y| < |x|$, is a subword of α. (In other words, xxc provides the shortest possible counterexample to Theorem 1.5.) If $|x|$ equals 1 or 2, one of the words a^3, b^3, $ababa$, $babab$ occurs as a subword of α. Since this is impossible by Lemma 1.3, we conclude that

$$|x| = t \geq 3. \tag{1.9}$$

Assume that the occurrence of xxc we are considering starts with the jth letter of α. Hence, in the notation of (1.7),

$$c_j \cdots c_{j+2t} = xxc. \tag{1.10}$$

By Lemma 1.3 and (1.9), either a^2 or b^2 occurs as a subword in xx. This implies that either a^2 or b^2 occurs twice as a subword in xxc. Indeed, a^2 or b^2 must occur as a subword either in x or else in xc. In both cases, it occurs twice as a subword in xxc.

We can now conclude by Lemma 1.4 that $|x| = t$ is even. For if t is odd then at least one of the occurrences of a^2 or b^2 in xxc must start with the kth letter of α, for some odd k. But this is impossible by Lemma 1.4.

Consequently, $t = 2u$ for some natural number u. We consider (1.10), assuming first that j is even and, hence, $j \geq 2$. We now apply our standard technique, choosing a large enough i (such that $|w_i| \geq j + 2t$) and making use of the relation $w_i = h(w_{i-1})$. We conclude that

$$c_{j-1}c_j = ab \text{ or } c_{j-1}c_j = ba. \tag{1.11}$$

This implies that also

$$c_{j-1+t}c_{j+t} = ab \text{ or } c_{j-1+t}c_{j+t} = ba \tag{1.12}$$

because $j + t$ is even. By (1.10), $c_j = c_{j+t}$ which together with (1.11) and (1.12) gives the result $c_{j-1} = c_{j-1+t}$. Consequently,

$$c_n = c_{n+t} \text{ for every } n \text{ with } j - 1 \leq n \leq j + t. \tag{1.13}$$

For $0 \leq n \leq t$, the word $c_{j-1+2n}c_{j+2n}$ equals either $h(a)$ or $h(b)$. This follows because of the relation $w_i = h(w_{i-1})$ and because $j - 1$ is odd. We now infer by (1.13) that w_{i-1} contains a subword yyd, where d is the first letter of y and $|y| = t/2 = u$. Hence, also α contains yyd as a subword. But this contradicts the choice of x.

Thus, there remains the case that in (1.10), j is odd. We argue as before, extending now (1.10) to the letter c_{j+2t+1} instead of c_{j-1}. Since both $j + t$ and $j + 2t$ are odd, the words $c_{j+t}c_{j+t+1}$ and $c_{j+2t}c_{j+2t+1}$ are of the form $h(a)$ or $h(b)$, analogously with (1.11) and (1.12). Hence, the equation $c_{j+t} = c_{j+2t}$ gives us the equation $c_{j+t+1} = c_{j+2t+1}$. Consequently,

$$c_n = c_{n+t} \text{ for every } n \text{ with } j \leq n \leq j + t + 1.$$

From this we obtain exactly as above the result that α contains a subword yyd, where d is the first letter of y and $|y| = u$, contradicting again the choice of x. We have shown that α is a strongly cube-free ω-word over the alphabet $\{a, b\}$, completing the proof of Theorem 1.5. $\qquad\square$

1.4 SOLUTION TO THE SQUARE-FREENESS PROBLEM

We now turn to the discussion of the problem of constructing a square-free ω-word over an alphabet with cardinality 3. In fact, we are able to reduce the entire matter to the already established Theorem 1.5. This becomes possible by applying a technique very common and useful in formal language theory. The technique consists of grouping several letters into one. By this technique, we obtain first the following lemma.

Lemma 1.6. There exists a square-free ω-word β over an alphabet with four letters.

Proof. Consider the ω-word α of Theorem 1.5. We define a new alphabet Σ_1 by

$$\Sigma_1 = \{[aa], [ab], [ba], [bb]\}.$$

Using the expression (1.7) for α, we now define an ω-word

$$\beta = d_1 d_2 d_3 \cdots \qquad (1.14)$$

over the alphabet Σ_1 by the condition

$$d_j = [c_j c_{j+1}] \text{ for every } j \geq 1.$$

Assume y^2 occurs as a subword in β where

$$y = d_{j+1} \cdots d_{j+t} = d_{j+t+1} \cdots d_{j+2t}, t \geq 1.$$

Consequently,

$$[c_{j+1}c_{j+2}] \cdots [c_{j+t}c_{j+t+1}] = [c_{j+t+1}c_{j+t+2}] \cdots [c_{j+2t}c_{j+2t+1}].$$

This means that $c_{j+1} = c_{j+t+1} = c_{j+2t+1}$ and that $c_{j+n} = c_{j+t+n}$ for $1 \leq n \leq t$. Consequently,

$$(c_{j+1} \cdots c_{j+t})^2 c_{j+1}$$

occurs as a subword in α, contradicting Theorem 1.5. Hence, β is square-free. $\square$

We now strengthen Lemma 1.6 to the result we are looking for. For this purpose it will be convenient to abbreviate the letters of Σ_1 as follows:

$$[aa] = 1, [ab] = 2, [ba] = 3, [bb] = 4.$$

In this notation, the beginning of β is

$$\beta = 2432312431232432312324312432312\ldots$$

(cf. 1.6). By the definition of β, the letter 1 must be preceded by 1 or 3. However, if 1 is preceded by 1 then a^3 occurs as a subword in α, which is impossible by Lemma 1.3. Hence, 1 is always preceded by 3 in β. The other parts of the following lemma are established in exactly the same way.

Lemma 1.7.   Every occurrence of the letter 1 in β is preceded by an occurrence of 3 and followed by an occurrence of 2. Every occurrence of the letter 4 in β is preceded by an occurrence of 2 and followed by an occurrence of 3.
    We are now ready for the main result.

Theorem 1.8.   There exists a square-free ω-word γ over an alphabet with three letters.

Proof.   Consider the alphabet $\Sigma_2 = \{1, 2, 3\}$. The ω-word γ is obtained from β by replacing 4 with 1. Thus, the beginning of γ is

$$\gamma = 2132312131232132312321312132312\ldots\ .$$

We will show that γ is square-free.
    Assume the contrary: xx occurs as a subword in γ, where x is a nonempty word. This implies that β contains a subword $y_1 y_2$ such that

$$|y_1| = |y_2| = |x| = t$$

and, furthermore, y_1 and y_2 become identical when every occurrence of the letter 4 is replaced by the letter 1.
    We observe first that $t \geq 2$ because, by Lemma 1.7, none of the words 11, 14, 41, 44 occurs as a subword in β.

Let

$$y_1 = d_{j+1} \cdots d_{j+t}, y_2 = d_{j+t+1} \cdots d_{j+2t},$$

where the notation of (1.14) is used. Thus, for every n satisfying $1 \le n \le t$, $d_{j+n} = d_{j+n+t}$ with the possible exception of the case where one of the numbers d_{j+n} and d_{j+n+t} equals 1 and the other equals 4. We shall prove that this exceptional case is, in fact, impossible.

Consider first a fixed value of n satisfying $1 \le n < t$. By Lemma 1.7, if d_{j+n} equals 1 (resp. 4), then d_{j+n+1} equals 2 (resp. 3). Hence, also $d_{j+n+1+t}$ equals 2 (resp. 3), by our assumption concerning y_1 and y_2. Thus, another application of Lemma 1.7 gives us the result

$$d_{j+n} = d_{j+n+t} \text{ whenever } 1 \le n < t. \tag{1.15}$$

Second, consider the letters d_{j+t} and d_{j+2t}. Instead of successors, we use now predecessors in our argument based on Lemma 1.7. If d_{j+t} equals 1 (resp. 4), then d_{j+t-1} equals 3 (resp. 2). Consequently, also d_{j+2t-1} equals 3 (resp. 2). Hence, $d_{j+t} = d_{j+2t}$, which combined with (1.15) shows that $(d_{j+1} \cdots d_{j+t})^2$ occurs as a subword in β, contradicting Lemma 1.6. Our assumption about xx occurring as a subword in γ is wrong, whence Theorem 1.8 follows. $\square$

We still summarize our complete solution of Thue's problem in the next theorem.

Theorem 1.9. If Σ is of cardinality ≥ 3 then there exists a square-free ω-word over Σ. If Σ is of cardinality 2 then there exists a strongly cube-free ω-word over Σ but no square-free words over Σ with length exceeding 3.

We want to emphasize that the expression "there exists" in the statement of the previous theorem means, in fact, that the required ω-word can be effectively constructed. By (1.5), we are able to compute any "digit" in α, β or γ. With very few exceptions, this is generally true in formal language theory: proofs of theorems give a method of effectively constructing the objects involved.

1.5   OVERLAPPING

By definition, a word or an ω-word w is square-free if it does not contain a subword of the form xx, where x is nonempty. It is still conceivable that w

could contain two "overlapping" occurrences of x, i.e., a subword $xy = zx$, where

$$1 \leq |y| = |z| < |x|. \tag{1.16}$$

If this does not happen, we say that w is *overlap-free*.

The following characterization result shows, among other things, that the square-free and strongly cube-free ω-words considered above are also overlap-free.

Lemma 1.10. A word or an ω-word w is overlap-free if and only if it is strongly cube-free.

Proof. Assume w is not overlap-free. Hence, w possesses a subword $xy = zx$ such that (1.16) holds. Let a be the first letter of z. By our assumptions, $x = zx_1$ where the first letter of x_1 is also a. Hence, zza is a subword of w. Consequently, w is not strongly cube-free.

Conversely, assume that w is not strongly cube-free. Hence, w possesses a subword z_1z_1a, where a is the first letter of z_1. Denoting $z_1 = az_2$, we see that az_2az_2a is a subword of w. We now choose

$$x = az_2a, y = z_2a, z = az_2.$$

Then $xy = zx$ is a subword of w and, moreover, (1.16) is satisfied. This implies that w is not overlap-free. $\square$

Thue also considered a notion stronger than square-freeness. He called an ω-word over Σ with cardinality n "irreducible" if, whenever it contains a subword xyx where x is nonempty, then $|y| \geq n - 2$. Thus, for $n = 3$, this notion coincides with the notion of square-freeness. Given any alphabet Σ, an irreducible ω-word over Σ can be constructed. (Observe that for $n \leq 2$ every ω-word is trivially irreducible.)

The condition of two occurrences of x lying apart can be further strengthened by requiring that the length of the word y separating the occurrences is bounded from below by $|x|$. Along these lines, the following result can be obtained.

Theorem 1.11. If Σ is of cardinality ≥ 3, there is an ω-word w over Σ such that, whenever xyx with $x \neq \lambda$ is a subword of w, then $|y| \geq \frac{1}{3}|x|$.

The proof of Theorem 1.11 is given in [De]. A w as required is generated by the DOL system $(\{a, b, c\}, h, a)$, where

$$
\begin{array}{llllllll}
h(a) = abc & acb & cab & c & bac & bca & cba, \\
h(b) = bca & bac & abc & a & cba & cab & acb, \\
h(c) = cab & cba & bca & b & acb & abc & bac.
\end{array}
$$

It is also discussed in [De] why $|h(a)|$ cannot be smaller and shown that the constant $\frac{1}{3}$ is the best possible in the following sense. Assume that the cardinality of Σ equals 3. Then every word over Σ with length ≥ 39 contains a subword xyx with the properties $x \neq \lambda$ and $|y| \leq \frac{1}{3}|x|$.

1.6 DOL SYSTEMS AND ω-WORDS

We conclude this chapter with some further examples of square-free ω-words. At the same time, some general remarks about ω-words generated by DOL systems will be made.

Observe first that the ω-word α of Theorem 1.5 is also generated by the DOL system

$$G_1 = (\{a, b\}, h, abba), \text{where } h(a) = ab, h(b) = ba,$$

as well as by the DOL system

$$G_2 = (\{a, b\}, h_1, a), \text{ where } h_1(a) = abba, h_1(b) = baab.$$

This is a special case of the following more general result, the proof of which is immediate by the definitions.

Lemma 1.12. Assume that δ is the ω-word generated by the DOL system (Σ, h, w) and that $i \geq 1$ and $j \geq 0$ are integers. Then δ is generated also by the DOL system $(\Sigma, h^i, h^j(w))$.

It may also happen that the original DOL system does not generate an ω-word, but there still exist numbers i and j such that the DOL system $(\Sigma, h^i, h^j(w))$ generates an ω-word. An example is given in Exercise 14. In Exercise 15 the problem of finding out whether or not such numbers exist is discussed.

In general, it is not easy to tell whether or not two DOL systems G_1 and G_2 (satisfying the additional condition for the generation of ω-words) generate the *same* ω-word. This problem is closely linked with the DOL sequence equivalence problem considered below in Chapter 5. If G_1 and G_2 are sequence equivalent (i.e., $S(G_1) = S(G_2)$), then they generate the same ω-word. The converse is not necessarily true, as exemplified by Lemma 1.12.

It is difficult to decide whether or not an ω-word defined by some other effective method can also be defined by a DOL system. This can be stated as a precise decision problem for each class of effective methods defining ω-words.

For instance, the ω-word β of Lemma 1.6 was not originally defined by a DOL system. However, β is generated by the DOL system $(\{1, 2, 3, 4\}, h, 2)$, where

$$h(1) = 2431, h(2) = 2432,$$
$$h(3) = 3123, h(4) = 3124.$$

No general method is known for deciding whether or not the ω-word generated by a DOL system G is square-free. In [Be1] such a method is given for the case where the alphabet of G consists of three letters.

We say that a morphism h *preserves square-freeness* if $h(x)$ is square-free whenever x is square-free. Clearly, the ω-word δ generated by the DOL system (Σ, h, w), where w is square-free and h preserves square-freeness, is itself square-free (providing, of course, that the conditions for generating an ω-word are satisfied). For instance, Thue shows in [T2] that the morphism h_1 defined by

$$h_1(a) = abcab, h_1(b) = acabcb, h_1(c) = acbcacb$$

is square-free. Thus, the DOL system $(\{a, b, c\}, h_1, a)$ generates a square-free ω-word.

However, a DOL system (Σ, h, w) may generate a square-free ω-word although h does not preserve square-freeness. An example is provided by the DOL system $(\{a, b, c\}, h_2, a)$, where h_2 is defined by

$$h_2(a) = abc, h_2(b) = ac, h_2(c) = b.$$

It can be shown that the generated ω-word is square-free. However, h_2 does not preserve square-freeness because

$$h_2(aba) = abcacabc.$$

EXERCISES

1. What is the number of subwords of a word w of length n, provided w contains no two occurrences of the same letter? Determine an upper bound, as sharp as possible, for the number of subwords in case the letters of w are not all distinct.

2. Consider the DOL system $G = (\{a, b\}, h, a)$, where $h(a) = b$ and $h(b) = ab$. Show that the lengths of the words in the sequence $S(G)$ constitute the Fibonacci sequence.

3. Instead of the definition given in the text, define a word or an ω-word to be strongly cube-free if it contains no subword of the form bx^2, where b is the last letter of x. Show that Theorem 1.9 remains valid. (This conclusion can be based on a really simple observation; you do not have to check through the proof.)

4. For a word w in Σ^*, define its *primitive root* $\rho(w)$ to be the shortest word u such that $w = u^n$ for some $n \geq 1$. Convince yourself that $\rho(w)$ is unique. Prove that $uw = wu$ if and only if $\rho(u) = \rho(w)$. Compare this result with Lemma 1.10.

5. Prove that if $u^m v^n = w^p$, where $m, n, p \geq 2$, then $\rho(u) = \rho(v) = \rho(w)$. (This result is due to [LyS].)

    Thue's construction can be applied in a variety of situations, arising in very different areas of study. A typical example is that it has been used to establish the existence of non-periodic recurrent motions in dynamics, [cf. MoH1]. The common denominator in such situations seems to be that one has to create something irregular out of a few given elements. Some further examples will be given in Exercises 6-8.

6. The conventional rules of chess contain rules about a draw by virtue of which every game contains only a finite number of moves. Various modifications to these rules about a draw have been proposed. One such modification is the following. The set of pawns and pieces on the board before a move constitutes a configuration, and there are only a finite number of different configurations. (It is understood that a configuration also contains information concerning which of the players is about to move.) A draw is proclaimed if any sequence of configurations is repeated twice in succession. (The conventional rule that a pawn be moved or a piece taken after a certain number of moves is dropped.)

    Show that an unending game is possible under this draw rule. More specifically, use in the argument only such configurations where each player has just the king left.

7. An element z is a *zero* in a semigroup S if $za = az = z$ holds for all elements a of S. The semigroup S is said to be *nilpotent* if there is an integer k such that $S^k = \{z\}$. Construct a non-nilpotent semigroup S generated by three elements such that the square of every element of S is zero.

8. Show that there are infinite groups which are finitely generated and in which every element has a finite order dividing an integer n. (Cf. [H].) (In fact, the Thue sequence is applied only in one part of the argument.)

9. Consider *idempotent* semigroups (in which every element a satisfies $a^2 = a$). Prove that every finitely generated idempotent semigroup is of finite order. (Cf. [Mc].) Contrast this result with Exercises 7 and 8.

10. Consider an ω-word $a_0 a_1 a_2 \ldots$ over the alphabet $\{a, b\}$ defined as follows. $a_n = a$ (resp. $a_n = b$) if there is an even (resp. odd) number of 1's in the expression of n as a binary number. Prove that this ω-word equals the ω-word of Theorem 1.5.

11. Consider "doubly infinite" words

$$\ldots c_{-2}c_{-1}c_0c_1c_2\ldots\ .$$

Give an example of a square-free doubly infinite word over the alphabet $\{a, b, c\}$ and of a strongly cube-free one over the alphabet $\{a, b\}$.

12. Is the ω-word γ of Theorem 1.8 generated by a DOL system? (Recall that γ was obtained by applying a length-preserving homomorphism to an ω-word β generated by a DOL system. ω-words obtained in this fashion are said to be generated by a "CDOL system.")

13. Consider the alphabet $\Sigma = \{0, 1, 2\}$ and the mappings f_1 and f_2 of Σ into Σ^3 defined by

$$f_1(0) = 012, f_1(1) = 120, f_1(2) = 201,$$

$$f_2(0) = 210, f_2(1) = 021, f_2(2) = 102.$$

Extend the domain of f_1 and f_2 to Σ^* by defining, for all a in Σ and w in Σ^*,

$$f_1(\lambda) = f_2(\lambda) = \lambda,$$

$$f_1(aw) = f_1(a) f_2(w), f_2(aw) = f_2(a) f_1(w).$$

Show that the sequence $f_1{}^i(0)$, $i = 0, 1, 2, \ldots$, defines a square-free ω-word. Show also that this ω-word is not generated by a CDOL system. (Cf. [Be2].)

14. The ω-*language* generated by a DOL system (Σ, h, w) consists of all ω-words δ such that δ is generated by some DOL system

$$(\Sigma, h^i, h^j(w)), i \geq 1, j \geq 0.$$

Consider the DOL system G of Exercise 2. Show that, although G itself does not generate an ω-word, the ω-language of G consists of two ω-words, none of which is cube-free. Do these ω-words contain subwords x^4, where x is not empty?

15. Assume that it is decidable whether two given DOL systems satisfying the additional condition for generating ω-words generate, in fact, the same ω-word. (In fact, the decidability of this question is open.) Show that, under this assumption, it is decidable whether or not two given DOL systems generate the same ω-language. (Here the result established in [Li3], according to which the emptiness of the ω-language generated by a DOL system is decidable, is very useful.)

16. A DOL system G is called *locally catenative* if its sequence

$$S(G) : w_0, w_1, w_2, \ldots$$

satisfies the following condition. There are positive integers t, i_1, ..., i_t such that

$$w_n = w_{n-i_1} \cdots w_{n-i_t}$$

holds for all sufficiently large n. (For instance, the DOL system of Exercise 2 is locally catenative with the formula

$$w_n = w_{n-2}w_{n-1}.)$$

Prove that the ω-language generated by a locally catenative DOL system is always nonempty and that it is decidable whether or not two given locally catenative DOL systems generate the same ω-language.

Chapter 2

REGULARITY: CHARACTERIZATIONS

2.1 REPRESENTABILITY

We now turn to the discussion of some very simple and natural devices for defining languages. It will be seen that some quite different-looking ones among such simple devices are equivalent in the sense that they define the same class of languages. This is shown in Kleene's Theorem. This beautiful theorem is still among the cornerstones of language theory. It characterizes the simplest widely studied class of languages, *regular* languages. It also fits very well in our general framework dealing with morphisms: it gives another characterization for languages obtainable by a simple morphic representation.

We define the notion of representability first in terms of (finite) directed graphs (shortly, digraphs) G. By definition, a *digraph* is a pair $G = (V, E)$, where V is a finite set whose elements are called *nodes* or *vertices* and E is a set of ordered pairs of elements of V. The elements of E are referred to as *edges* or *arrows*.

In the sequel we consider *labeled* digraphs: one or several letters of an alphabet Σ are associated with each edge. Furthermore, two (not necessarily disjoint) subsets of V are specified, referred to as the set of *initial* and the set of *final* nodes. A labeled digraph, where initial and final nodes have been specified, is also referred to as a *finite automaton*. An example of such a finite automaton G_1 over the alphabet $\Sigma = \{a, b\}$ and with six nodes and six edges is the following one:

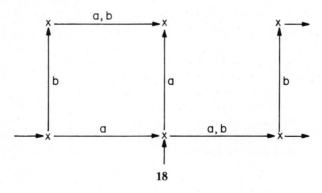

The initial (resp. final) nodes are marked by small incoming (resp. outgoing) arrows.

For any finite path in a labeled digraph, we obtain one or several associated words by reading the labels along the path. The occurrence of several words depends on whether some edge in the path is labeled by two or more letters. Returning to our example, each of the words

$$a, b, ab, bb, aa, aab, abb \tag{2.1}$$

is attached to a path from an initial to a final node. Indeed, the word ab is attached to two different such paths. (We have omitted the formal definition of a path and an associated word, but the readers might want to define these notions themselves.)

We now introduce the most important notion in these considerations. The language $L(G)$ *represented* by a finite automaton G over Σ consists of all words w over Σ such that w is attached to some path from an initial node to a final node in G. A path containing no edges is considered to be labeled by the empty word λ. Consequently, λ is in $L(G)$ if and only if some initial node is also a final node.

Thus, the words (2.1) belong to the language $L(G_1)$ represented by our example automaton G_1. It is easy to see that, in fact, $L(G_1)$ consists of the words (2.1). Thus, in this case, $L(G_1)$ is a finite language. For the finite automaton G_2 defined by the digraph

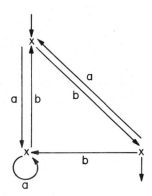

we see immediately that $L(G_2)$ is infinite because it contains, for instance, all words of the form $a^i b^2$ with $i \geq 1$. The reader might try to characterize the language $L(G_2)$. Although the automaton has just three nodes, such a characterization is not quite immediate.

A language L is called *representable* if there is a finite automaton G such that

$$L = L(G).$$

It is very easy to see, cf. Exercise 1, that all finite languages are representable. On the other hand, for instance, the language

$$L = \{a^i b^i \,|\, i \geq 1\}$$

is not representable. Intuitively, a finite automaton is able to "count" only up to the number of its nodes and, consequently, cannot generate L. A more formal argument considers an arbitrary finite automaton G satisfying $L(G) = L$. If i is greater than the number of nodes in G, then any path from an initial to a final node labeled by $a^i b^i$ passes twice through some node. But this means that there is a number $j < i$ such that $a^j b^i$ is in $L(G)$, a contradiction.

Kleene's Theorem established below gives an exhaustive characterization of representable languages. Before presenting this theorem, we discuss some equivalent definitions of representability whose equivalence to the definition given above is rather immediate.

Given an alphabet Σ and a positive integer n, consider a mapping h of Σ into the set of $n \times n$ matrices whose entries equal either 0 or 1. The domain of h is extended to Σ^* by the conventions that $h(\lambda)$ is the identity matrix and

$$h(w_1 w_2) = h(w_1)h(w_2)$$

holds for arbitrary words w_1 and w_2. (The juxtaposition on the right side of the equation denotes matrix multiplication.) Thus, h becomes a morphism of Σ^* into the multiplicative semigroup of $n \times n$ matrices. Consider, further, n-dimensional row and column vectors π and ζ with all entries equal to 0 or 1.

Given a word w in Σ^*, we form the product

$$\pi h(w)\zeta. \tag{2.2}$$

Clearly, the product (2.2) is a nonnegative integer for any w. Those words w for which the product (2.2) is positive constitute a language over Σ, referred to as the language *represented by the triple* (h, π, ζ). A language L is said to possess a *matrix representation* if it is represented by some triple (h, π, ζ), where h, π and ζ are as above for some value of n.

Lemma 2.1. A language L is representable if and only if it possesses a matrix representation.

Proof. Given a finite automaton G over the alphabet Σ, we construct a triple (h, π, ζ) as follows. The dimension n equals the number of nodes in G. Furthermore, we consider an (arbitrary but fixed) ordering of the nodes. For any $i = 1, \ldots, n$, the ith entry in π (resp. ζ) equals 1 if and only if the ith node in G is an initial (resp. a final) one. If i and j are positive integers $\leq n$ and a is an element of Σ then the (i, j)th entry in the matrix $h(a)$ equals 1 if and only if there is an arrow labeled by a in G from the ith node to the jth node.

Conversely, we can attach in exactly the same way a finite automaton to a given triple (h, π, ζ). Thus, we obtain a one-to-one correspondence between finite automata G and triples (h, π, ζ). Furthermore, we claim that this correspondence preserves the represented languages: if $L = L(G)$ and L_1 is represented by the triple (h, π, ζ) corresponding to G then $L = L_1$.

Our claim is established by showing inductively that, for every $k \geq 0$, both L and L_1 contain the same words of length k. This is true for $k = 0$: both L and L_1 contain λ exactly in case some initial node of G is also a final node. Assume, as an inductive hypothesis, that both L and L_1 contain the same words of length less than k. Let w be a word of length k. We write w in the form $w = w_1 a$, where a is a letter. Then the following statements (i)-(v) are equivalent:

  (i) w is in L_1.
 (ii) $(\pi h(w_1))(h(a)\zeta)$ is positive.
(iii) w_1 is in the language represented by the triple (h, π, ζ') where ζ' is obtained from $h(a)\zeta$ by replacing positive entries with the number 1.
 (iv) w_1 is in the language represented by the finite automaton G' obtained from G by changing the final nodes to those corresponding to ζ'.
  (v) w is in L.

In particular, the equivalence between (iii) and (iv) follows by the inductive hypothesis (more specifically, by applying the inductive hypothesis to G' and the triple (h, π, ζ')). The equivalences between (i) and (ii), (ii) and (iii), and (iv) and (v) follow by the definitions and the rule for matrix multiplication.

Consequently, we have completed the inductive step, and the lemma follows.   □

Another rather immediately equivalent definition of representability is obtained by considering right-linear grammars. For future purposes, we now also define the more general notion of a grammar, as well as different types of grammars.

A *rewriting system* is a pair (Σ, P), where Σ is an alphabet and P is a finite set of ordered pairs of words over Σ. The elements (w, u) of P are referred to as *rewriting rules* or *productions* and denoted by $w \to u$. Given a rewriting system, the *yield relation* $\Rightarrow$ on the set Σ^* is defined as follows. For any words x and y, $x \Rightarrow y$ holds if and only if there are words x_1, x_2, w, u such that

$$x = x_1 w x_2, y = x_1 u x_2$$

and $w \to u$ is a production in the system. The reflexive transitive closure of the relation $\Rightarrow$ is denoted by $\Rightarrow^*$. (Thus $x \Rightarrow^* y$ holds if and only if there are $n \geq 1$ words $x_1, \ldots, x_n$ such that $x = x_1, y = x_n$ and $x_i \Rightarrow x_{i+1}$ holds for every $i = 1, \ldots, n - 1$.)

A (*phrase structure*) *grammar* is a quadruple $G = (R, \Sigma_N, \Sigma_T, \Sigma_S)$ where $R = (\Sigma, P)$ is a rewriting system, Σ_N and Σ_T are disjoint alphabets such that $\Sigma = \Sigma_N \cup \Sigma_T$, and Σ_S is a subset of Σ_N. The elements of Σ_N, Σ_T and Σ_S are referred to as *nonterminal*, *terminal* and *start* letters, respectively. The language *generated* by the grammar G is defined by

$$L(G) = \{w \in \Sigma_T^* \mid S \Rightarrow^* w \text{ for some } S \in \Sigma_S\}.$$

(Here $\Rightarrow^*$ is the relation determined by the rewriting system R.)

For $i = 0, 1, 2, 3$, the grammar G is of *type i* if the restrictions (i) on the production set P, as given below, are satisfied:

(0) No restrictions.
(1) Each production in P is of the form $w_1 A w_2 \to w_1 w w_2$, where w_1 and w_2 are arbitrary words over Σ, w is a nonempty word over Σ, and A belongs to Σ_N (with the possible exception of the production $S \to \lambda$, $S \in \Sigma_S$, whose occurrence in P implies, however, that S does not occur on the right side of any production).
(2) Each production is of the form $A \to w$ with A in Σ_N.
(3) Each production is of the form $A \to aB$, where $A, B \in \Sigma_N$ and $a \in \Sigma_T$, or of the form $A \to \lambda$, where $A \in \Sigma_N$.

A language is of *type i*, $i = 0, 1, 2, 3$, if it is generated by a grammar of type i.

It can be shown that the resulting four families of languages constitute a strictly decreasing hierarchy of language families, usually referred to as the *Chomsky hierarchy*. Type 0 languages are also called *recursively enumerable*. Type 1 (resp. type 2, type 3) grammars and languages are also called *context-sensitive* (resp. *context-free, right-linear*). As the purpose of this book is not to go into a systematic study of the hierarchy, the interested reader is referred to [Sa2].

For the language class studied in this chapter, right-linear grammars are of special interest, as seen in the following lemma.

Lemma 2.2.   A language is representable if and only if it is of type 3.

Proof.   The lemma follows rather immediately from the definitions. As in the proof of the previous lemma, it is straightforward to construct a one-to-one correspondence between the two classes of definitional devices. We just briefly indicate this construction.

Given a finite automaton H with the set of nodes Σ_N and the alphabet of labels Σ_T, we construct a right-linear grammar G as follows. Σ_N and Σ_T are the nonterminal and terminal alphabets. The alphabet Σ_S consists of all initial nodes. The production $A \rightarrow aB$ is in G if and only if there is an arrow labeled by a from A to B in H. Furthermore, the production $A \rightarrow \lambda$ is in G if and only if A is a final node in H. There are no further productions in G. Clearly, in exactly the same way we can construct H, starting from G. The construction preserves the defined language.   □

2.2   FINITE DETERMINISTIC AUTOMATA

We consider now a further characterization of representability. We show that a subclass of finite automata suffices to define the entire family of representable languages. The automata in this subclass are very convenient to work with.

A finite automaton is called a *finite deterministic automaton* if, for each node A and each label a in the label alphabet, there is exactly one arrow emanating from A labeled with a and, furthermore, there is exactly one initial node. Observe that G_2 discussed above is a finite deterministic automaton.

Lemma 2.3.   A language is representable if and only if it is represented by a finite deterministic automaton.

Proof.   The "if"-part being obvious, we show that every representable language is represented by a finite deterministic automaton. Thus, consider a language $L = L(G)$ represented by a finite automaton G. Our aim is to construct a finite deterministic automaton G' such that $L = L(G')$. The technique applied is often quite useful: the subset construction.

We define first the set of nodes of G'. There is a one-to-one correspondence between the set of nodes of G' and the set of subsets of the node set of G (including the empty subset). For simplicity, we identify the nodes of G' with the subsets mentioned. The initial node of G' is the subset consisting of all initial nodes of G. A node M of G' is final if and only if it contains (viewed as a subset of the set of nodes of G) a final node of G. The alphabet of labels for arrows of G' equals that of G. For any node M of G' and any letter a of the label alphabet, there is in G' an arrow labeled by a from M to the node

$\{x \mid$ there is in G a node labeled by a from some node in M to $x\}$.

It follows from the definition that G' is a finite deterministic automaton. Furthermore,

$$L(G) = L(G')$$

holds because whenever there is a path from an initial node s_0 to a final node s_1, in G, labeled by a word w, then there is also a path labeled by w in G' from the initial node to a final node containing s_1, and conversely. This follows by the very construction. Observe, in particular, the role of the empty set ϕ as a node of G'. It acts as a "garbage" node: whenever it is entered, it cannot be left. $\square$

In most cases the finite deterministic automaton G' constructed in the previous proof will be unnecessarily big: the same language is represented by a finite deterministic automaton G'' with fewer nodes. Such a G'' with a minimal number of nodes is unique (up to isomorphism) and is easy to construct from G', cf. Exercise 2.

We summarize in the following theorem the results obtained so far.

Theorem 2.4. The following conditions (i)-(iv) are equivalent for a language L.

  (i) L is representable.
 (ii) L possesses a matrix representation.
(iii) L is represented by a finite deterministic automaton.
(iv) L is of type 3.

We have so far not motivated our terminology. Why are certain labeled digraphs called automata? Although we do not want to enter into a systematic discussion of automata theory, the following remarks are still in order. Consider a finite deterministic automaton. It can be viewed as a machine with a finite number of internal *states*, represented symbolically by the nodes. The different labels for the arrows are different *inputs*. The digraph indicates the behavior of the machine, showing into which new state it enters after being in a certain state and receiving a certain input. The machine is always started in the initial state. The final states may be viewed as accepting ones: if a word *w* causes a sequence of state transitions from the initial to one of the final states, it is accepted by the machine. Otherwise, it is rejected. Therefore, finite deterministic automata are often called finite-state acceptors. Instead of a digraph, a transition table (that is, a two-place function describing the state transitions) can also be used to define the automaton.

In the same way, finite automata can be viewed as *nondeterministic* machines: for each configuration, there may be several possibilities for the behavior (or no possibilities whatsoever). A word *w* is accepted exactly in case it causes a sequence of state transitions from an initial state to a final one: all eventual failures are disregarded if there is one successful sequence of moves caused by *w*. Theorem 2.4 tells us that the accepting capacity of finite deterministic automata equals that of finite nondeterministic automata.

Representable languages possess the very useful property that one can give algorithms for the solution of practically every question asked about them. This property is not any more true of context-free languages, not to speak of the languages in the two highest classes in the Chomsky hierarchy. The following theorem presents some results easily obtainable at this stage.

Theorem 2.5. The complement of a representable language is representable. There is an algorithm for deciding whether or not a given representable language is (i) empty, (ii) infinite.

Proof. Consider the first sentence. By Theorem 2.4, any representable language L over Σ is represented by a finite deterministic automaton G. Clearly, the complement of L (i.e., the set of words in Σ^* not belonging to L) is represented by the finite deterministic automaton obtained from G by making all final states non-final, and vice versa.

Consider the second sentence. Given a finite automaton G, we can easily decide whether there is a path from an initial node to a final one and, consequently, we can find out whether or not $L(G)$ is empty. (More specifically, we consider first the set S_0 of initial nodes of G, then the set S_1 consisting of nodes to which there is an edge from a node in S_0, then the set S_2 consisting of nodes to which there is an edge from a node in S_1, and so forth. The procedure terminates either when we reach a final node or else when some S_i

contains no new nodes, i.e., no nodes not belonging to any S_j with $j < i$.) The infinity of $L(G)$ is decided similarly: $L(G)$ is infinite if and only if there is a path from an initial node to a final node having the following additional property. Some node b in the path possesses a loop, i.e., there is a path (with at least one edge) from b to b.   □

Regarding the preceding proof, the reader is also referred to Exercise 4.

2.3   REGULAR EXPRESSIONS

Various *operations* defined for languages are important in formal language theory. Languages being sets, we may immediately define the Boolean operations of *union, intersection*, and *complementation*. For two languages L_1 and L_2, $L_1 \cup L_2$ and $L_1 \cap L_2$ denote their set-theoretic union and intersection, respectively. If L_1 is a language over the alphabet Σ but not over any proper subalphabet of Σ (i.e., Σ is the minimal alphabet of L_1), then the *complement* $\sim L_1$ of L_1 consists of all words in Σ^* not belonging to L_1. (If we want the complement to be unique, we have to specify the alphabet because any language over Σ is also a language over an arbitrary alphabet containing Σ. In fact, such a specification was tacitly assumed in the proof of Theorem 2.5.)

The *catenation* (or *product*) of two languages L_1 and L_2 is defined by

$$L_1 L_2 = \{w_1 w_2 \,|\, w_i \text{ in } L_i, \text{ for } i = 1, 2\}.$$

Catenation is clearly an associative operation and, consequently, the customary power notation L^i can be used for $i \geq 1$. Furthermore, L^0 is defined to be the language $\{\lambda\}$.

The *catenation closure* L^* of a language L is defined to be the union of all powers L^i where $i \geq 0$. Thus, a word w is in L^* if and only if either $w = \lambda$ or else w is obtained by catenating an arbitrary finite number of words in L.

The three operations—union, catenation, and catenation closure—are referred to as *regular operations*. Given an alphabet Σ, the empty language ϕ and each language $\{a\}$, where a is in Σ, are called *atomic* languages over Σ. A language over Σ is *regular* if it is obtained from atomic languages by finitely many applications of regular operations. A *regular expression* is a formula telling how a specific language is obtained from atomic languages by regular operations.

More explicitly, a regular expression over Σ is defined recursively as follows.

(i) ϕ and every letter a of Σ is a regular expression over Σ.

(ii) If α and β are regular expressions over Σ, then so are $(\alpha \cup \beta)$, $(\alpha\beta)$ and α^*.

(iii) All regular expressions over Σ are obtained by (i) and (ii).

Every regular expression over Σ denotes a language over Σ in the obvious fashion: ϕ denotes the empty language, a the language $\{a\}$, $(\alpha \cup \beta)$ the union of the languages denoted by α and β, $(\alpha\beta)$ their catenation, and α^* the catenation closure of the language denoted by α. For instance, the regular expression $a(bb)^*$ denotes the language $\{ab^{2i} \mid i \geq 0\}$. (We omit unnecessary parentheses from regular expressions. The order of precedence of the operations is the customary one from algebra: catenation closure binds strongest and catenation stronger than union.)

Regular operations and languages are sometimes also referred to as *rational* because the operations resemble the familiar rational operations. In the theory of formal power series (cf. [SalS]) this resemblance becomes very explicit.

We have defined two families of languages, representable and regular languages, by quite different means: the former by a device recognizing certain words and the latter by a recursive construction. Kleene's Theorem tells us that, in fact, these two families coincide. We establish the inclusion of the family of regular languages in that of representable languages first.

Lemma 2.6. The family of representable languages is closed under regular operations. Consequently, every regular language is representable.

Proof. The second sentence follows from the first because, clearly, all atomic languages are representable.

Consider the first sentence. Assume that L_1 and L_2 are representable languages. By Lemma 2.2, we may assume that $L_i = L(G_i)$, where G_i is a type 3 grammar, for $i = 1, 2$. Since the nonterminals can always be renamed without affecting the generated language, we may further assume that the nonterminal alphabets of G_1 and G_2 are disjoint.

It is now easy to construct, for each of the languages

$$L_1 \cup L_2 = L_3, \quad L_1 L_2 = L_4, \quad L_1^* = L_5$$

a type 3 grammar G_i generating the language L_i, for $i = 3, 4, 5$. In fact, G_3 is obtained from G_1 and G_2 simply by taking the union of all items: nonterminal, terminal, and start letters, as well as productions.

The terminal (resp. nonterminal) alphabet of G_4 consists of the union of the terminal (resp. nonterminal) alphabets of G_1 and G_2. The start letters of G_4 are those of G_1. The production set of G_4 consists of

(i) the productions of G_2,
(ii) the productions of G_1 except those of the form $A \rightarrow \lambda$, and
(iii) for each production $A \rightarrow \lambda$ of G_1 and each production $B \rightarrow \alpha$ of G_2 where B is a start letter, the production $A \rightarrow \alpha$.

Finally, the productions of G_5 consist of those of G_1 and, in addition,

(i) for each production $A \rightarrow \lambda$ and each production $B \rightarrow \alpha$ of G_1 where B is a start letter, of the production $A \rightarrow \alpha$, and
(ii) of the production $B' \rightarrow \lambda$ where B' is a new start letter added to the alphabet of G_1.

(Observe that (ii) is needed to make sure that λ is in the generated language.)
Lemma 2.6 now follows by Lemma 2.2. $\square$

By Theorem 2.5 and Lemma 2.6 (and the fact that intersection can be expressed in terms of union and complement), we now obtain the following result.

Theorem 2.7.   The family of representable languages is closed under Boolean operations.

Observe that our proof of Theorem 2.7 has been effective: if L is obtained by Boolean operations from representable languages $L_1, \ldots, L_n$ and a finite automaton defining L_i is given, for $i = 1, \ldots, n$, then a finite automaton defining L can be constructed.

Clearly, for any languages L_1 and L_2, $L_1 = L_2$ holds if and only if

$$\sim L_1 \cap L_2 = L_1 \cap \sim L_2 = \phi.$$

By Theorem 2.5, we can decide the emptiness of a representable language. Consequently, we also obtain the following result.

Theorem 2.8.   There is an algorithm for deciding whether or not two given finite automata represent the same language.

Theorem 2.8 is quite remarkable because algorithms for deciding equivalence are not common for language defining devices. For instance, it will be seen in Chapter 5 that no such algorithm exists for context-free grammars.

2.4 KLEENE'S THEOREM

We shall now prove that the families of regular and representable languages coincide.

Theorem 2.9. A language is representable if and only if it is regular.

Proof. By Lemma 2.6, it suffices to prove that every representable language is regular. By Lemma 2.3, it suffices to prove that every language represented by a finite deterministic automaton is regular.

Assume that $L = L(G)$, where G is a finite deterministic automaton with $n \geq 1$ nodes $q_1, \ldots, q_n$, the initial node being q_1. For

$$1 \leq i \leq n, 1 \leq j \leq n, \text{ and } 0 \leq k \leq n,$$

we denote by $L(i, j, k)$ the collection of the labeling words of all such paths in G from q_i to q_j which do not pass through any node q_t with $t > k$. (It is understood by definition that $\lambda \in L(i, j, k)$ if and only if $i = j$.)

For any i and j, the language $L(i, j, 0)$ either is empty or else is the union of some of the languages $\{\lambda\}$ and $\{a\}$, where a ranges through the alphabet of $L(G)$. Hence, for any i and j, the language $L(i, j, 0)$ is regular. (Observe that $\{\lambda\}$ is denoted by the regular expression ϕ^*.)

Proceeding inductively, we assume that for a fixed value k, where $0 \leq k \leq n - 1$, each of the languages $L(i, j, k)$ is regular. Since obviously, for any i and j,

$$L(i, j, k + 1) = L(i, j, k) \cup L(i, k + 1, k)L(k + 1, k + 1, k)^*L(k + 1, j, k),$$

we conclude that each of the languages $L(i, j, k + 1)$ is regular. Consequently, by induction, each of the languages $L(i, j, n)$ is regular.

But the language $L = L(G)$ equals the union of languages $L(1, j, n)$ such that q_j is a final node of G. Therefore, L is regular. $\square$

Observe again that all arguments used in the proof of Theorem 2.9 are effective: if a regular expression is given for a language L, then a finite automaton (or a finite deterministic automaton) representing L can be constructed, and vice versa. Thus, because of Theorem 2.8, there is an algorithm for deciding whether or not two given regular expressions denote the same language. We want to emphasize that the algorithms resulting from the proofs above are not the most practical ones. In specific situations, *ad hoc* arguments or the algorithms given, for instance, in [Sa1] are in general more convenient.

We mention, finally, that quite different looking regular expressions may denote the same language. The reader might want to verify that the regular expressions

$$(ab^*c)^* \quad \text{and} \quad \phi^* \cup a(b \cup ca)^*c,$$

as well as the regular expressions

$$(ba \cup a^*ab)^*a^* \quad \text{and} \quad (a \cup ab \cup ba)^*$$

denote the same language.

EXERCISES

1. Show that every finite language is representable. (Show this directly from the definition: of course it is an immediate consequence of Kleene's theorem.)

2. Define the *weight* of a regular language L, in symbols weight(L), to be the smallest number of nodes in a finite deterministic automaton representing L. Construct an algorithm for finding weight(L), as well as the corresponding minimal automaton. Show that the latter is unique up to isomorphism. (A trivial but in practice very complicated algorithm is to make a systematic search through all automata smaller than the given one and apply Theorem 2.8. A more practical algorithm can be found, for instance, in [Sa1].)

3. Define the *representation number* of a regular language L, in symbols repr(L), to be the smallest number of final nodes in a finite deterministic automaton representing L. Show by examples that repr(L) can be arbitrarily large. Study algorithms of finding weight(L) and repr(L) when L is a finite language. (Cf. [Sa1].)

4. Show that a regular language represented by a finite deterministic automaton with n nodes is infinite if and only if it contains a word w such that $n \leq |w| < 2n$. Establish also the following "pumping lemma." Every sufficiently long word w in a regular language L can be written in the form $w = tuv$, where $u \neq \lambda$ and $tu^iv \in L$ for all $i = 0, 1, 2, \ldots$.

5. Let L be any language whatsoever over the alphabet $\{a\}$. Prove that L^* is regular.

6. Consider the product (2.2) where the items are defined as in the proof of Lemma 2.1. Show that the product equals the numbers of distinct paths from an initial to a final node, labeled by the word w.

7. Let L be a language over the alphabet Σ. The *equivalence relation* $\equiv_L$ *induced by* L is the binary relation on the set Σ^* defined by the condition: $u \equiv_L v$ holds if

and only if there is no word w such that exactly one of the words uw and vw is in L. Show that L is regular if and only if the index (i.e., the number of equivalence classes) of $\equiv_L$ is finite. Show also that the index of $\equiv_L$ equals weight (L). (There is quite an extensive literature concerning the relation $\equiv_L$. For instance, [Ei], [Sa1] and [Sa2] contain more information.)

8. Consider equations $\alpha = \beta$ between regular expressions α and β, meaning that α and β denote the same language. There is a great variety of valid equations, some of them describing simple properties of union and catenation, others indicating more involved relations between the star and the other operations. For instance, all of the following equations, where α, β, and γ are arbitrary regular expressions, are valid:

$$\alpha \cup (\beta \cup \gamma) = (\alpha \cup \beta) \cup \gamma,\ \alpha(\beta\gamma) = (\alpha\beta)\gamma,$$
$$\alpha \cup \beta = \beta \cup \alpha,\ \alpha(\beta \cup \gamma) = \alpha\beta \cup \alpha\gamma,$$
$$(\alpha \cup \beta)\gamma = \alpha\gamma \cup \beta\gamma,\ \phi^*\alpha = \alpha,$$
$$\phi\alpha = \phi,\ \alpha^* = \alpha^*\alpha \cup \phi^*,$$
$$\alpha^* = (\alpha \cup \phi^*)^*.$$

New valid equations can be obtained from given ones by uniform substitution for the letters, and by the following rule of inference: from the equation $\alpha = \alpha\beta \cup \gamma$ one may infer the equation $\alpha = \gamma\beta^*$, provided the language denoted by β does not contain the empty word. Show that all valid equations are obtained in this fashion. (Cf. [Sa1] and [Sa2], as well as [MiS] for a recent generalization of this result.)

9. Investigate ω-languages associated with finite deterministic automata. More specifically, we can generalize the notion introduced in Exercise 1.14 as follows. For any language L, the corresponding ω-language consists of ω-words α such that infinitely many prefixes of α are in L. What can you say about ω-languages associated with regular languages? (For detailed information, consult [Ei].)

10. Show that each of the ω-words considered in connection with Thue's problem (Theorems 1.5 and 1.8, Lemma 1.6) appears in the ω-language associated with some regular language. Show also that such an ω-language necessarily contains ω-words also with arbitrarily high powers x^i as subwords. (This is the reason why DOL systems are essentially better than finite automata for dealing with Thue's problem.)

11. Study closure properties of the families of regular, context-free, and recursively enumerable languages with respect to Boolean and regular operations. (For a general survey of closure properties, see [Sa2].) In particular, show that the intersection of two context-free languages is not necessarily context-free but that the intersection of a context-free and a regular language is context-free. (Hint. The last fact is established by a "triple construction" which is often very useful in language theory: nonterminals are triples (p, α, q), where α is a letter of the given grammar, and p and q are nodes of the given automaton. These triples are

used to simulate both derivations according to the grammar and transitions according to the automaton. For instance, the production $A \to BC$ becomes the set of productions $(p, A, q) \to (p, B, q_1)(q_1, C, q)$, where p and the q's are arbitrary. Productions $(p, a, q) \to a$ are added in case there is in the automaton an arrow labeled by a from p to q. The set of start symbols consists of nonterminals of the form (q_0, S, q_F), where q_0 is the initial node, q_F is a final node, and S is a start symbol.)

Chapter 3

REGULARITY: CHALLENGING PROBLEMS

3.1 STAR HEIGHT

The simplest devices for language definition, regular expressions (or finite automata) and DOL systems, have been the source of mathematically interesting and intriguing problems. Many people—and this writer is certainly one of them—prefer problems easily explainable even to a person who does not know anything of the area to problems in which the main difficulty consists of understanding the notions involved. A typical example of the first type of problem is Fermat's conjecture. For obvious reasons, we do not want to even hint at an example of the second type of problem.

Thus, regular expressions and DOL systems have been the source of many problems classified above as the first type. In fact, in spite of numerous attempts at solution, many of these problems are still open.

In this chapter, we present the solution of two problems dealing with regular languages. Both are tricky enough, so that the readers can be congratulated if they are able to work out a solution themselves. Both problems concern the star operator. The star operator is the essence of the theory. Union and catenation alone define only finite languages. However, the combination of the star operator with union and catenation may lead to some difficult questions.

We begin by introducing the notion of star height. Essentially, the star height of a regular expression is the greatest number of nested stars in the expression, i.e., the length of the longest chain of stars within stars. The star height of a regular language L is the star height of the "most economical" regular expression α for L, i.e., among the regular expressions denoting L no one possesses a smaller star height than α.

Definition. The *star height of a regular expression* α over the alphabet Σ, in symbols $sh(\alpha)$, is a nonnegative integer defined recursively as follows.

(i) The letters of Σ and ϕ have star height 0.

(ii) If $sh(\alpha) = i$ and $sh(\beta) = j$, then $sh((\alpha \cup \beta)) = sh((\alpha\beta)) = max(i, j)$.

(iii) If $sh(\alpha) = i$, then $sh(\alpha^*) = i + 1$.

The *star height of a regular language* L, in symbols $sh(L)$, is the least integer i such that $sh(\alpha) = i$, for some regular expression α denoting L.   □

The star height indicates the "loop complexity" of a regular expression: an expression with lower star height is less complex although it might be longer in terms of the number of symbols. Can the star height of every regular expression be "reduced" below some bound by choosing another regular expression denoting the same language? In other words, is the star height of every regular language over Σ always less than some constant which possibly depends on the cardinality of Σ? This is the first problem we want to study in this chapter.

An immediate observation is that in many cases the star height of a given regular expression can indeed be reduced. For any regular expression α, both α^* and $(\alpha^*)^*$ denote the same language. A less trivial example is provided by the two pairs of regular expressions

$$(ab^*c)^* \text{ and } \phi^* \cup a(b \cup ca)^*c,$$
$$(ba \cup a^*ab)^*a^* \text{ and } (a \cup ab \cup ba)^*$$

mentioned at the end of Chapter 2. In both cases, we have a reduction of the star height from 2 to 1. Clearly, the star height cannot be further reduced because no infinite language is of star height 0.

The following theorem gives an example of a class of regular expressions whose star height can be drastically reduced.

Theorem 3.1.   Every regular language L over a one-letter alphabet $\Sigma = \{a\}$ is of star height one at most.

Proof.   By Theorems 2.9 and 2.4, we may assume that $L = L(G)$, where G is a finite deterministic automaton whose label alphabet equals $\{a\}$. But such a G can always be depicted as follows:

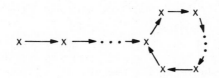

This means that the set of integers

$$\{i \,|\, a^i \text{ is in } L\},$$

ordered according to increasing magnitude, is ultimately periodic. If the period equals p, we conclude that

$$L = F_1 \cup F_2\{a^p\}^*, \tag{3.1}$$

where F_1 and F_2 are finite languages over $\{a\}$. The right side of (3.1), viewed as a regular expression, is of star height 1. Consequently, the star height of L is at most 1.   □

The intuitive idea behind Theorem 3.1 is that, when considering a one-letter alphabet, the length of the words is the only thing that matters and, consequently, stars within stars become unnecessary. This conclusion is not any more true when alphabets with two or more letters are considered. In fact, our purpose is to establish the following result.

Theorem 3.2.   There are regular languages with any preassigned star height over any alphabet containing at least two letters.

The proof of Theorem 3.2 consists of showing that a certain language L_i, denoted by a regular expression α_i with star height i, cannot be denoted by any regular expression with a star height smaller than i. The regular expressions α_i are defined for all values of $i \geq 1$.

We first make some initial observations. To prove the theorem, we need only to show that there are regular expressions with any preassigned star height ≥ 1 over the alphabet $\{a, b\}$. This consequence follows because a regular expression over $\{a, b\}$ is also a regular expression over any alphabet containing $\{a, b\}$ and because, for instance, $\{a\}$ is a regular language with star height 0 over $\{a, b\}$.

The regular expressions α_i, $i = 1, 2, \ldots$, are defined recursively as follows:

$$\alpha_1 = (ab)^*,$$
$$\alpha_i = (a^{2^{i-1}}\alpha_{i-1}b^{2^{i-1}}\alpha_{i-1})^*, i \geq 2.$$

Thus, for instance,

$$\alpha_3 = (a^4(aa(ab)^*bb(ab)^*)^*b^4(aa(ab)^*bb(ab)^*)^*)^*.$$

Now let L_i be the regular language denoted by α_i, for $i = 1, 2, \ldots$. For completion of the proof of Theorem 3.2, it suffices to show that the star height of L_i equals i, for every i. Because clearly the star height of α_i equals i, for every i, we conclude that

$$sh(L_i) \leq i.$$

Hence, it suffices to show that

$$sh(L_i) \geq i, \text{ for every } i \geq 1. \tag{3.2}$$

In the proof of (3.2) auxiliary words $w(i, j)$, where $i, j \geq 1$, over the alphabet $\{a, b\}$ will be very useful. The words are defined recursively as follows:

$$w(1, j) = ab, \text{ for all } j \geq 1;$$

$$w(i, j) = a^{2^{i-1}}(w(i-1, j))^j b^{2^{i-1}}(w(i-1, j))^j,$$

for all $i \geq 2$ and $j \geq 1$. Thus, for instance,

$$w(3, 2) = a^4(aaababbbabab)^2 b^4(aaababbbabab)^2.$$

For any word w over the alphabet $\{a, b\}$, denote by $\#_a(w)$ the number of occurrences of the letter a in w. The notation $\#_b(w)$ is defined in the same way. Thus,

$$\#_a(w(3, 2)) = \#_b(w(3, 2)) = 28.$$

We now consider a fixed value of $i \geq 1$ and define K_i to be the family of regular languages L over $\{a, b\}$ satisfying the following three conditions:

(i) There is an integer t such that every word w in L satisfies

$$\#_a(w) = \#_b(w) + t.$$

(ii) There are infinitely many values of j such that $(w(i, j))^j$ occurs as a sub-word in at least one word of L.

(iii) L is of minimal star height satisfying (i) and (ii), i.e., there is no regular language L' satisfying (i) and (ii) and with the property

$$sh(L') < sh(L).$$

We will first make several preliminary observations concerning the families K_i. Clearly, for every i, the language L_i satisfies the conditions (i) (with $t = 0$) and (ii). (In fact, that L_i satisfies (ii) follows by an obvious induction on i: for $i = 1$ the statement is clear, and the inductive step is accomplished by the definition of α_i and $w(i, j)$.) This shows that the family K_i is nonempty, for every $i \geq 1$. Moreover, condition (iii) guarantees that the languages in K_i possess a common star height d_i. Because $sh(L_i) \leq i$ and L_i satisfies (i) and (ii), we conclude that

$$d_i \leq sh(L_i) \leq i, \text{ for all } i \geq 1. \tag{3.3}$$

Clearly, every language satisfying (ii) must be infinite. This fact implies that we cannot have $d_1 = 0$ and consequently, by (3.3),

$$d_1 = 1. \tag{3.4}$$

We consider now an arbitrary but fixed $i \geq 2$ and an arbitrary language L in K_i. Because $sh(L) = d_i$, we conclude that L is a finite union of languages, each of which is denoted by a regular expression of the form

$$\beta = \gamma_0^*\gamma_1\gamma_2^* \cdots \gamma_{2n-1}\gamma_{2n}^*, \tag{3.5}$$

where the star height of each of the regular expressions $\gamma_j, j = 0, \ldots, 2n$, is at most $d_i - 1$. (Note that γ_0 or γ_{2n} may reduce to the regular expression ϕ.) Furthermore, the language denoted by β satisfies condition (i) because L itself satisfies (i). We may also assume that the language denoted by β in (3.5) satisfies condition (ii). (This result follows because L satisfies (ii) and, consequently, one language in the union defining L must satisfy (ii). We let (3.5) denote that language.)

In order to prove Theorem 3.2, we shall now establish three lemmas.

Lemma 3.3. None of the languages denoted by the regular expressions γ_u, $u = 0, \ldots, 2n$, in (3.5) satisfies condition (ii).

Proof. Assume the contrary: for some u, the language L' denoted by γ_u satisfies (ii). We claim that L' satisfies also (i). This follows because the language denoted by β satisfies (i) and, by the definition of β, there are words w_1 and w_2 such that w_1ww_2 is in the language denoted by β whenever w is in L'.

But because L' satisfies (i) and (ii) and is of smaller star height than L, we conclude that L does not satisfy (iii). This contradiction proves Lemma 3.3.

Lemma 3.4.   There exists an integer u, $0 \leq u \leq n$, such that the language denoted by $\gamma_{2u}{}^*$ in (3.5) satisfies condition (ii).

Proof.   Assume the contrary. Then, by Lemma 3.3, none of the languages denoted by the regular expressions

$$\gamma_0{}^*, \gamma_1, \gamma_2{}^*, \ldots, \gamma_{2n-1}, \gamma_{2n}{}^* \tag{3.6}$$

satisfies condition (ii). The fact that the number of these languages is finite implies the existence of an integer j_0 such that, whenever $j > j_0$, then the word $(w(i,j))^j$ is not a subword of any word belonging to one of the languages denoted by the regular expressions (3.6).

By Theorem 2.9, the language denoted by the regular expression β is represented by a finite deterministic automaton G. Let j_1 be the number of nodes of G. Because the language L_β denoted by the regular expression β satisfies condition (ii), there is an integer

$$j_2 > max(j_0, j_1) \tag{3.7}$$

such that $(w(i,j_2))^{j_2}$ is a subword of some word in L_β. Consequently, there are words w_1 and w_2 such that the word

$$w_1(w(i,j_2))^{j_2}w_2$$

is in L_β. Now by (3.7) j_2 exceeds the number of nodes of G. This implies the existence of integers m_1 and m_2, $1 \leq m_1 < m_2 \leq j_2$, such that the words

$$w_1(w(i,j_2))^{m_1} \text{ and } w_1(w(i,j_2))^{m_2}$$

lead the automaton G to the same node from the initial node. Denoting $m = m_2 - m_1$, we conclude that the words

$$w_1(w(i,j_2))^{j_2+tm}w_2, \tag{3.8}$$

where t is an arbitrary nonnegative integer, are in L_β.

Recalling the definition of j_0 and L_β, we infer that none of the words

$$(w(i,j_2))^j, \; j > (2n + 1)j_2,$$

is a subword of a word in L_β. (Otherwise, the word $(w(i,j_2))^{j_2}$ would be a subword of a word in some of the languages denoted by the regular expressions

(3.6).) But this conclusion contradicts the fact that all of the words (3.8) are in L_β. $\square$

Lemma 3.5. There exists an integer u, $0 \le u \le n$, such that the language $L^{(2u)}$ denoted by γ_{2u} in (3.5) satisfies the following condition (modified from (ii)): there are infinitely many values of j such that $(w(i - 1, j))^j$ occurs as a subword in at least one word of $L^{(2u)}$.

Proof. We claim that the integer u from Lemma 3.4 satisfies also Lemma 3.5. Again, assume the contrary: there is a natural number j_0 such that, whenever $j > j_0$, then the word $(w(i - 1, j))^j$ does not occur as a subword in any word in $L^{(2u)}$.

By Lemma 3.4, $(L^{(2u)})^*$ satisfies condition (ii). Consequently, there is an integer $j_1 > j_0$ such that the word

$$(w(i, j_1))^{j_1} = (a^{2^{i-1}}(w(i - 1, j_1))^{j_1} b^{2^{i-1}}(w(i - 1, j_1))^{j_1})^{j_1}$$

is a subword of some word in $(L^{(2u)})^*$. Hence, also the word $w(i, j_1)$ is a subword of some word in $(L^{(2u)})^*$. This implies the existence of an integer v and words $w_1, \ldots, w_v$ in $L^{(2u)}$ such that

$$w(i, j_1) = a^{2^{i-1}}(w(i - 1, j_1))^{j_1} b^{2^{i-1}}(w(i - 1, j_1))^{j_1} \tag{3.9}$$

is a subword of the word $w_1 \cdots w_v$.

As seen above in the proof of Lemma 3.3, the language $L^{(2u)}$ satisfies condition (i). But also the language $(L^{(2u)})^*$ satisfies condition (i) because the language L_β denoted by β satisfies (i). Moreover, because the empty word is in $(L^{(2u)})^*$, this language must satisfy condition (i) with $t = 0$. This implies that also $L^{(2u)}$ satisfies condition (i) with $t = 0$.

Consequently, in each of the words

$$w_1, \ldots, w_v \tag{3.10}$$

the number of occurrences of a equals that of b. Recall that (3.9) is a subword of $w_1 \cdots w_v$. We now investigate how this is possible.

Let p, $1 \le p < v$, be the integer such that the first occurrence of

$$(w(i - 1, j_1))^{j_1} \tag{3.11}$$

in (3.9) begins in w_p (when we consider some fixed occurrence of (3.9) as a subword of $w_1 \cdots w_v$). Let q be the integer such that the first occurrence of

(3.11) ends in w_q. Then $q > p$ because if $q = p$ then (3.11) occurs as a sub-word in w_p, which is impossible by the definition of j_0 and the choice of j_1. This implies that we can write

$$w_q = xy, \qquad (3.12)$$

where x is a proper suffix of (3.11).

It now follows by the definition of the words $w(i, j)$ that (1) no suffix of (3.11) contains more a's than b's, and (2) every prefix of the word

$$b^{2^{i-1}}(w(i - 1, j_1))^{j_1} \qquad (3.13)$$

(including the word itself) contains more b's than a's.

Since w_q contains equally many a's and b's, the conditions (1) and (2) imply that y in (3.12) must be the empty word λ. Consequently, the word (3.13) is a prefix of the word $w_{q+1} \cdots w_v$. But this outcome is possible, because of condition (2), only if (3.13) is a prefix of w_{q+1}. Because $j_1 > j_0$, this again contradicts the choice of j_0. The contradiction proves the correctness of Lemma 3.5.   □

We are now in the position to prove (3.2) and, therefore, Theorem 3.2 also.

By Lemma 3.5, the language $L^{(2u)}$ satisfies the conditions (i) and (ii)$'$, where (ii)$'$ results from (ii) by considering $i - 1$ instead of i. This implies the inequality

$$d_{i-1} \le sh(L^{(2u)}). \qquad (3.14)$$

On the other hand, we saw that in (3.5) the language denoted by one of the regular expressions γ is of star height at most $d_i - 1$. Consequently, also

$$sh(L^{(2u)}) \le d_i - 1. \qquad (3.15)$$

Since $i \ge 2$ was arbitrary, (3.14) and (3.15) imply that

$$d_i \ge d_{i-1} + 1 \text{ for all } i \ge 2. \qquad (3.16)$$

The inequality (3.2) is now an immediate consequence of (3.3), (3.4), and (3.16).   □

Although Theorem 3.2 gives an answer to one of the basic problems concerning star height (the problem of constructing languages with an arbitrary preassigned star height), many other basic problems concerning star height are still open. The most famous among them, often referred to as "the star height problem," consists of finding an algorithm to determine the star height of an arbitrary regular language. In spite of results like Theorem 2.8, none of the numerous efforts to solve this problem has so far been successful. Related matters are also discussed in Exercise 1.

3.2   FINITE POWER PROPERTY

In the second part of this chapter we discuss another rather tricky problem about regular languages. The problem remained open for quite a long time before it was finally settled in the late 1970's.

We say that a regular language L possesses the *finite power property* (in short, FPP) if the set

$$\{L^i | i = 0, 1, 2, \dots\}$$

is finite.

A related notion is defined as follows. The *order* of a regular language L is the smallest integer k satisfying

$$L^k = L^{k+1};$$

if no such k exists we say the order of L is ∞.

The following simple lemma deals with the interconnections between the notions just defined.

Lemma 3.6.   The following conditions (i)–(iii) are equivalent for a nonempty regular language L: (i) L possesses FPP; (ii) there is an integer k such that L is of order k; (iii) there is an integer k such that $L^k = L^*$.

Proof.   First observe that each of the conditions (i)–(iii) implies that λ is in L because, otherwise, for all integers i, the shortest word in L^i is shorter than the shortest word in L^{i+1}. Hence, each of the conditions (i)–(iii) also implies that, for all integers i, $L^i \subseteq L^{i+1}$. From this result the equivalence of conditions (i)–(iii) immediately follows. Observe, in particular, that condition (ii) implies that $L^k = L^{k+i}$ holds for all integers i. $\square$

We will mention some simple examples. No finite language L containing a nonempty word possesses FPP. Hence, such an L is of infinite order. This conclusion follows immediately from the fact that, for all integers i, the longest word in L^{i+1} is longer than the longest word in L^i.

Every star language, i.e., a regular language of the form L^*, possesses FPP. In fact, the order of such a language equals 1. Less trivial examples are provided by the language L_1 denoted by the regular expression

$$\lambda \cup a^2(a^3)^*,$$

as well as by the language L_2 denoted by the regular expression

$$(\lambda \cup b^*a)(b \cup ab^*ab^*a)^*.$$

Both L_1 and L_2 possess FPP. The reader might want to verify that the order of L_1 equals 3, whereas that of L_2 equals 2.

The *FPP problem* consists of giving an algorithm for deciding of an arbitrary regular language L whether or not L possesses FPP. In view of Theorems 2.8, 2.9, and Lemma 3.6, it is clear that this problem is equivalent to the problem of giving a method of finding the order of an arbitrary regular language L.

Although some special cases of the FPP problem are relatively easy to settle (cf. Exercises 3–5), the solution of the problem in its full generality turned out to be quite difficult and was completed only very recently. The remainder of this chapter is devoted to the presentation of this solution.

We define first a notion which will provide intuitive background for the subsequent arguments. This is the only purpose of the notion; the arguments can be carried out without using it.

Given a finite deterministic automaton G, we define the *iterate G^** of G to be the following (in general nondeterministic) finite automaton. The set of nodes of G^* equals that of G added with a node denoted by I (for "iterate"). The initial and final nodes, as well as the alphabet of labels, in G^* equal the corresponding items in G. (Thus, in particular, I is not a final node.) All arrows of G are present also in G^*. In addition, G^* has the following arrows to and from the new node I. Whenever there is an arrow in G from a node q to a final node, labeled by a, then there is an arrow in G^* labeled by a from q to I. Whenever there is an arrow labeled by a in G from the initial node to a node q, then there is an arrow in G^* labeled by a from I to q and, moreover provided that q is a final node, an arrow labeled by a from I to I.

For instance, if G is the finite deterministic automaton

then G^* is defined by the graph

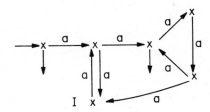

As before, we mark initial (resp. final) nodes by small incoming (resp. outgoing) arrows. Observe that G represents the language L_1 discussed above and denoted by the regular expression $\lambda \cup a^2(a^3)^*$.

Lemma 3.7. $(L(G))^* = L(G^*) \cup \{\lambda\}$.

Proof.   The result is an immediate consequence of the definition of G^*. Consider a word $w \neq \lambda$ in $(L(G))^*$. It can be. written as

$$w = x_1 \cdots x_n, \, x_i \in L(G) \text{ for } i = 1, \ldots, n.$$

For $i < n$, there is a path in G^* from the initial node to I labeled by $x_1 \cdots x_i$ and, consequently, we can start all over again in G, showing that w is in $L(G^*)$. On the other hand, whenever there is a path in G^* from the initial node to I labeled by w, then w is in $(L(G))^*$. This fact is easy to establish inductively. It also shows, by the definition of G^*, that every word in $L(G^*)$ is in $(L(G))^*$. Observe that λ is not necessarily in $L(G^*)$ and, hence, that it has to be added as a separate term in the union. $\square$

Given a word w, there are in general several paths in G^* which begin from the initial node and are labeled by w. Considering such paths, we now focus our attention to the number of times the special node I is visited.

The *iteration number* of a word $w \in L(G^*)$, in symbols $IN(w)$, is the smallest integer k such that there is in G^* a path labeled by w from the initial node to a final node, and passing k times through the node I.

For instance, if G is the example automaton considered above we observe that

$$IN(a^5) = 0, \, IN(a^4) = 1, \, IN(a^6) = 2.$$

It can be shown that in this case $IN(a^i) \leq 2$, for any i.

Clearly, the iteration number is defined with respect to a previously fixed G. We use the simpler notation $IN(w)$ (rather than $IN_G(w)$) because G will always be clear from the context. The same remark applies also to several other notions defined below.

In what follows we denote $L(G) = R$. Thus, $R^* = L(G^*) \cup \{\lambda\}$. We also assume that R contains a nonempty word.

Lemma 3.8.   Assume that w is a nonempty word in R^* and that $IN(w) = k$. Then w is in R^{k+1} but not in any R^i with $i < k + 1$.

Proof.   By the definition of G^*, w can be expressed as

$$w = x_1 \cdots x_{k+1}, x_j \text{ in } R.$$

Thus, w is in R^{k+1}.

Assume w can be written as

$$w = y_1 \cdots y_i, i < k + 1, y_j \text{ in } R. \tag{3.17}$$

Because G represents R, we obtain by (3.17) a path in G^* from the initial to a final node and labeled with w but passing only $i - 1$ times through the node I. Since $i - 1 < k$, this condition contradicts the fact that $IN(w) = k$.   □

Lemma 3.8 shows also that, given R and w in R^*, $IN(w)$ is independent of the automaton representing R.

We have already pointed out that because G^* is nondeterministic, given a word w, there may be several paths starting with the initial node of G^* and labeled by w. Moreover, these paths do not have to end at the same node. This leads us to define $START(w)$ to be the set of nodes $q \neq I$ in G^* such that there is a path in G^* from the initial node to q labeled by w.

Thus, $START(w)$ is the set of possible end points of the paths labeled by w. Observe that we want the paths to end in "G proper" because we require $q \neq I$. $START(w)$ is defined for all words w (not only for those in R^*).

Similarly, $END(w)$ is defined to be the set of all nodes $q \neq I$ in G^* such that there is a path in G^* from q to one of the final nodes labeled by w.

To illustrate the notion of the set $START(w)$ further, we point out that it can be defined without using the iterate G^* as follows. (Thus, we are given only G and $L(G) = R$.) $START(w)$ equals the set of nodes q in G such that, for some decomposition $w = w_1 w_2$ where w_1 is in R^*, there is a path from the initial node of G to q labeled by w_2. Similarly, $END(w)$ can be defined as the set of nodes q in G such that either there is a path from q to a final node labeled by w, or else, for some decomposition $w = xyz$, the following conditions (i)–(iii) are satisfied: (i) there is a path from q to a final node labeled by x; (ii) y is in R^*; and (iii) there is a path from the initial node to a final node labeled by z (i.e., z is in R). Observe that $START(\lambda)$ consists of the initial node and $END(\lambda)$ of all final nodes.

The following result is an immediate consequence of Lemma 3.7 and the definition of $START(w)$ and $END(w)$.

Lemma 3.9. Assume that a nonempty word w in R^* can be decomposed as $w = w_1 w_2$. Then

$$START(w_1) \cap END(w_2) \tag{3.18}$$

is nonempty. Conversely, whenever (3.18) is nonempty for a word $w = w_1 w_2$, then w is in R^*.

So far our notions and lemmas have not dealt directly with FPP. The next lemma does so and is also an important tool in the subsequent discussion.

Lemma 3.10. Assume that $w = xyz$ is a nonempty word in R^* such that

$$START(x) = START(xy) \text{ and } END(z) = END(yz). \tag{3.19}$$

Then if R possesses FPP, there are nodes q and q' in

$$START(x) \cap END(z) \tag{3.20}$$

(possibly $q = q'$) such that there is a path in G from q to q' labeled by y.

Proof. Observe first that, by (3.19) and Lemma 3.9, the intersection (3.20) is nonempty.

We establish the lemma indirectly, assuming that whenever q and q' are in (3.20), then there is no path from q to q' labeled by y. (Recall that a path containing no edges is considered to be labeled by λ.) It is a consequence of (3.19) that

$$START(x) = START(xy^i) \text{ and } END(z) = END(y^j z),$$

for all i and j. This fact implies by Lemma 3.9 that $xy^i z$ is in R^* for every i. On the other hand, our assumption implies that, for all i,

$$IN(xy^i z) \geq i. \tag{3.21}$$

(To see this result, we argue more specifically as follows. Consider a path p labeled by x from the initial node to a node in (3.20). In order to continue p with a path labeled by y and still end up at a node in (3.20), we must pass through I. The same applies to every copy of y and, hence, (3.21) follows.)

But now (3.21) and Lemma 3.8 imply that, for any k, we can find a word in R^* which is not in R^k. This conclusion contradicts the fact that R possesses FPP.   □

The intuitive meaning of Lemma 3.10 is the following. If R possesses FPP, we want to show that there is a number k, computable from the automaton G alone, with the property $R^k = R^*$. To this end, we want to show that every word w in R^* is in R^k. Writing w in the form $w = xyz$ such that (3.19) holds, we are looking for an $i \leq k$ such that w is in R^i. Now Lemma 3.10 shows that the subword y increases the exponent i we are looking for by at most one, because the path labeled by y is in G and, consequently, does not pass through I.

We now present this argument in detail. For this purpose, we need a few additional notions. We use $\#S$ to denote the cardinality of a finite set S.

The *order* of a word w in R^* is defined by

$$o(w) = min\{k \mid w \in R^k\}.$$

Furthermore, for w in R^* we define

$$PAIRS(w) = \{(S, S') \mid w = xy, START(x) = S,$$
$$END(y) = S', \text{ for some } x \text{ and } y \text{ (possibly empty)}\},$$

and

$$WORST(w) = (i, j), \text{ where}$$
$$i = max\{\#S + \#S' \mid (S, S') \text{ in } PAIRS(w)\},$$
$$j = \#\{(S, S') \text{ in } PAIRS(w) \mid \#S + \#S' = i\}.$$

Thus, $PAIRS(w)$ gives all possible pairs of sets of nodes obtained by decomposing w in different ways. The first component in $WORST(w)$ indicates the maximal number i obtained by summing up the cardinalities of the two sets in some element of $PAIRS(w)$, and the second component indicates the number j of times this maximal number is reached.

If $w \neq \lambda$, then (by Lemma 3.9) both sets in every element of $PAIRS(w)$ are nonempty. Thus, $i \geq 2$. Denoting by n the total number of nodes of G, we obtain the bounds

$$2 \leq i \leq 2n. \tag{3.22}$$

Moreover,

$$1 \leq j \leq \binom{2n}{i}.$$

Letting b_n be the greatest among the binomial coefficients $\binom{2n}{i}$, where $2 \leq i \leq 2n$, we obtain

$$1 \leq j \leq b_n. \tag{3.23}$$

Observe that the estimate $j \leq \binom{2n}{i}$ could be slightly improved by taking into account the fact that both sets in every element of $PAIRS(w)$ are non-empty. However, we are not looking for the best bounds but prefer simpler ones. This remark applies also in other parts of the present argument.

We now consider pairs (i, j) such that (3.22) and (3.23) are satisfied. An ordering $\leq$ among such pairs is defined in the "lexicographic" way: $(i_1, j_1) \leq (i_2, j_2)$ holds if either $i_1 < i_2$, or else $i_1 = i_2$ and $j_1 \leq j_2$.

The following notation is used for i and j satisfying (3.22) and (3.23) in case R possesses FPP:

$$o(i,j) = max\{o(w) \,|\, w \in R^* \text{ and } WORST(w) \leq (i,j)\},$$
$$o(i) = o(i, b_n).$$

We assume that R possesses FPP because, otherwise, the maximum does not necessarily exist. We observe the convention that $o(i, j) = 1$ if there is no w in R^* such that $WORST(w) \leq (i, j)$. Similarly, $o(i) = 1$ if there is no w in R^* such that $WORST(w) \leq (i, b_n)$, i.e., there is no w in R^* such that the first component of $WORST(w)$ is $\leq i$. These conventions guarantee that $o(i, j)$ and $o(i)$ are defined for all i and j satisfying (3.22) and (3.23).

It is a direct consequence of the definitions that, whenever $(i_1, j_1) \leq (i_2, j_2)$, then also $o(i_1, j_1) \leq o(i_2, j_2)$. This monotonicity result holds for the one-place operator as well: whenever $i_1 \leq i_2$, then also $o(i_1) \leq o(i_2)$. Moreover, if R possesses FPP, then $o(w) \leq o(2n)$, for all words w in R^*.

Our purpose is to show that there is a number c_n, computable effectively from the number n of nodes in G, such that

$$o(2n) \leq c_n, \tag{3.24}$$

provided R possesses FPP. This allows us to decide whether or not a given R possesses FPP: we construct G and test whether or not

$$R^{c_n} = R^*.$$

The following lemma is the most important tool in the proof of (3.24).

Lemma 3.11.   Assume that R possesses FPP and that $i \geq 3$ and $j \geq 2$ are numbers satisfying (3.22) and (3.23). Then

$$o(i, j) \leq o(i - 1) + o(i, j - 1) + 3. \tag{3.25}$$

Proof.   If there is no word w in R^* such that $WORST(w) = (i, j)$, then $o(i, j) = o(i, j - 1)$. Consequently, (3.25) is satisfied.

Hence, to prove the lemma, we need only to show that an arbitrary w with the property $WORST(w) = (i, j)$ satisfies

$$o(w) \leq o(i - 1) + o(i, j - 1) + 3. \tag{3.26}$$

(Observe that this procedure also takes care of the case, where the order of every word w with $WORST(w) = (i, j)$ is, in fact, less than or equal to $o(i, j - 1)$.) Let us now consider an arbitrary but fixed w with $WORST(w) = (i, j)$. We may assume that $w \neq \lambda$ because $o(\lambda) = 0$. (In fact, (3.26) is immediately satisfied if $|w| \leq 5$.)

We now write w in the form $w = xz_1$, where

$$\#(START(x)) + \#(END(z_1)) = i$$

and, moreover, x is the shortest prefix of w with this property. (In other words, whenever $w = x'z_1'$ and

$$\#(START(x')) + \#(END(z_1')) = i,$$

then $|x| \leq |x'|$.) We denote

$$START(x) = S, END(z_1) = S'.$$

We next write z_1 in the form $z_1 = yz$, where

$$START(x) = START(xy) = S \text{ and } END(yz) = END(z) = S'$$

and, moreover, z is the shortest suffix of z_1 with this property. (In other words, whenever $z_1 = y'z'$ and

$$START(x) = START(xy') \text{ and } END(y'z') = END(z'),$$

then $|z| \leq |z'|$.)

Thus, $w = xyz$. It is possible that one or two of the words x, y, and z equal λ.

By Lemma 3.10, there are nodes q and q' in $S \cap S'$ such that there is a path from q to q' labeled by y in G. We now extend this path to a path from the initial node to a final one as follows.

Let u be a suffix of x such that there is a path in G from the initial node to q labeled by u. Similarly, let v be a prefix of z such that there is a path in G from q' to a final node labeled by v. (More specifically, the paths labeled by u and v are assumed to be subpaths of the path labeled by $w = xyz$.) Thus

$$x = w_1u, \; z = vw_2, \; w = w_1uyvw_2,$$

for some words w_1 and w_2 in R^*. The existence of u and v is guaranteed by the fact that w is in R^*. Moreover, uyv is in R. It is possible that one or both of the words u and v are empty.

Because uyv is in R and clearly always $o(w'w'') \leq o(w') + o(w'')$, we obtain

$$o(w) \leq o(w_1) + 1 + o(w_2). \tag{3.27}$$

If $u \neq \lambda$, the choice of x guarantees that $o(w_1) \leq o(i - 1)$. (Clearly, if a decomposition of w_1 would yield the maximal number i, then i could be reached in w already before x.) If $u = \lambda$ and $w_1 \neq \lambda$, we write w_1 $(=x)$ in the form $w_1 = w_3w_4$, where w_3 is in R^* and $w_4 \neq \lambda$ is in R. This shows that

$$o(w_1) \leq o(i - 1) + 1. \tag{3.28}$$

Since (3.28) clearly holds also for $w_1 = \lambda$, we conclude that (3.28) holds true in all cases.

If $v \neq \lambda$, the choice of z guarantees that $o(w_2) \leq o(i, j - 1)$. (More specifically, all maximal pairs, with total cardinality i, obtainable from decompositions of w_2, are obtainable from decompositions of w; but the particular pair (S, S') is not obtainable from a decomposition of w_2.) If $v = \lambda$ and $w_2 \neq \lambda$, we write w_2 $(=z)$ in the form $w_2 = w_5w_6$, where w_6 is in R^* and $w_5 \neq \lambda$ is in R. This shows that

$$o(w_2) \leq o(i, j - 1) + 1. \tag{3.29}$$

Since (3.29) again clearly holds for $w_2 = \lambda$, we conclude that it is valid in all cases.

But now (3.26) is a direct consequence of (3.27)-(3.29). Hence, the lemma follows.   □

Lemma 3.12.   Assume that R possesses FPP and that $i \geq 3$ satisfies (3.22). Then

$$o(i, 1) \leq 2o(i - 1) + 3.$$

Proof.   Exactly as the previous lemma except that now, when considering w_2, $o(i - 1)$ rather than $o(i, j - 1)$ appears in the upper bound.   □

Recall that we are trying to find an upper bound for $o(2n)$. The previous lemmas give a method of reduction. We still need an estimate for the "low end," i.e., for the situation where the reduction has been completed.

Lemma 3.13.   If R possesses FPP, then $o(2) \leq 1$.

Proof.   If there are no words w in R^* such that the first component in $WORST(w)$ equals 2, the result $o(2) = 1$ follows by the definition of $o(2)$.

Consider an arbitrary $w \neq \lambda$ in R^* such that the first component in $WORST(w)$ equals 2. This condition implies by Lemma 3.9 that, for any decomposition $w = w_1 w_2$, $START(w_1) = END(w_2)$ consists of exactly one node. Consequently, for any path p labeled by w in G^* starting from the initial node and passing (one or several times) through the node I, there is a path labeled by w in G starting from the initial node and ending at the same node as p. This means that w is in R and, hence, $o(w) = 1$. Since $o(\lambda) = 0$, the lemma follows.   □

In Lemma 3.13 the assumption that R possessed FPP was made only because this state was assumed in our definition of $o(i)$. Otherwise (i.e., if the definition of $o(i)$ is generalized), the argument in the proof of the lemma does not use this assumption. We are now ready to establish the main result.

Theorem 3.14.   Assume that R is a regular language represented by a finite deterministic automaton with n nodes. Then there is an integer c_n, effectively computable from n, such that R possesses FPP if and only if

$$R^{c_n} = R^*. \tag{3.30}$$

Consequently, the FPP problem is decidable. Moreover, there is an algorithm for determining the order of a given regular language.

Proof.   Assume that R possesses FPP. Successive applications of Lemma 3.11 give us first, for any i such that $3 \leq i \leq 2n$,

$$o(i) = o(i, b_n) \leq o(i - 1) + 3 + o(i, b_n - 1)$$
$$\leq 2(o(i - 1) + 3) + o(i, b_n - 2) \leq \cdots$$
$$\leq (b_n - 1)(o(i - 1) + 3) + o(i, 1).$$

Hence, applying Lemma 3.12 we obtain

$$o(i) \leq (b_n + 1)(o(i - 1) + 3) \leq 4(b_n + 1)o(i - 1).$$

We denote now

$$a_n = 4(b_n + 1) \text{ and } c_n = a_n^{2n-2}.$$

Consequently, for $3 \leq i \leq 2n$,

$$o(i) \leq a_n o(i - 1).$$

Hence,

$$o(2n) \leq a_n o(2n - 1) \leq a_n^2 o(2n - 2) \leq \cdots$$
$$\leq a_n^{2n - 2} o(2).$$

This yields by Lemma 3.13

$$o(2n) \leq c_n. \tag{3.31}$$

Since the order of every word w in R^* is at most $o(2n)$, (3.30) is an immediate consequence of (3.31).

We have shown that if R possesses FPP, then (3.30) holds. Clearly, if R does not possess FPP, then (3.30) does not hold. Consequently, we can solve the FPP problem as follows. Given R (by means of G), we first compute c_n. We then test whether or not (3.30) holds. This proof can be done by Theorem 2.8.

The order of a given regular R can now be determined as follows. We first decide by the method given above whether or not R possesses FPP. If R does not possess FPP, it is of infinite order by Lemma 3.6. Otherwise, we test for $k = 0, 1, 2, \ldots$, whether or not

$$R^k = R^{k+1}. \tag{3.32}$$

This sequence of tests terminates because R possesses FPP. The order of R is the smallest k satisfying (3.32). $\square$

We conclude this chapter with another interesting characterization of FPP. The condition in this characterization (the existence of a particular word) is decidable also by a method not using the results given above. The reader is referred to [Li1] for details.

Theorem 3.15.   A nonempty regular language R is of infinite order if and only if there is a word w in R^* such that, for all $i \geq 1$, $w^i \notin R^i$.

Proof.   The "if" part is clear. (Observe that whenever w is in R^*, then so is w^i for all i.) To prove the "only if" part, assume that R is of infinite order. Then there is a word xyz in R^* such that

$$START(x) = START(xy) \text{ and } END(yz) = END(z)$$

and moreover, whenever q and q' are nodes in

$$S = START(x) \cap END(z) \quad (S \neq \phi),$$

then there is no path in G (the finite deterministic automaton representing R) from q to q' labeled by y. This proof is seen as follows. The only consequence of the FPP used in the proof of Lemma 3.11 and in the subsequent argument leading to the estimate $o(2n) \leq c_n$ is the conclusion of Lemma 3.10. Hence, the converse of Lemma 3.10 is also valid: if R does not possess FPP, then there is a word xyz in R^* such that (3.19) is satisfied but that the statement about (3.20) is not satisfied.

As in the proof of Lemma 3.10 we now conclude that, for all i, xy^iz is in R^* and

$$IN(xy^iz) \geq i. \tag{3.33}$$

Moreover for any q in S, there is a path in G^* (but not in G) from q to some node in S labeled by y. The fact that S is finite implies that there are a node q in S, a decomposition $y = y_1y_2$, and an integer m such that there is in G^* a path from q to a final node (resp. from the initial node to q) labeled by y_1 (resp. $y_2 y^m$). Consequently, $y_2 y^m y_1 = (y_2 y_1)^{m+1}$ is in R^*.

Denote now $t = 2|xyz|$ and define

$$w = (y_2 y^m y_1)^t.$$

The word w is in R^* because $y_2 y^m y_1$ is in R^*.

To see that w satisfies the required condition, we assume the contrary: for some $i \geq 1$, w^i is in R^i. Then the word

$$xy^{i(m+1)t+1}z = xy_1(y_2 y_1)^{i(m+1)t}y_2 z = xy_1 w^i y_2 z$$

is in $R^{i+|xyz|}$. But this result contradicts (3.33) and Lemma 3.8 because

$$i(m+1)t + 1 = 2i(m+1) \cdot |xyz| + 1$$

$$> |xyz| + i(m+1) \cdot |xyz| \geq |xyz| + i. \qquad \square$$

We mention finally that the bound c_n obtained in Theorem 3.14 is quite huge in view of the fact that no examples are known of regular languages of order greater than n (the number of nodes in the representing automaton) which still possess FPP.

EXERCISES

1. In a *generalized regular expression* also intersection and complementation may be used, the definition being otherwise the same as the one given in Chapter 2. Show that the language L denoted by the regular expression $(ababa)^*$ is also denoted by a *star-free* generalized regular expression, i.e., L is obtained from the languages ϕ, $\{a\}$, $\{b\}$ by finitely many applications of catenation and Boolean operations. (Languages denoted by star-free generalized regular expressions coincide with noncounting languages, cf. [McP].) By definition, a regular language L is *noncounting* if there is an integer n such that, for all words x, y, z, we have $xy^n z \in L$ exactly in case $xy^{n+1}z \in L$. For instance, $\{ab, ba\}^*$ is noncounting but $\{a^2\}^*$ is not noncounting. We mention, finally, that the notion of star height can be extended in the natural way to concern generalized regular expressions. Then it is not known whether or not there exist languages with star height ≥ 2.

2. By an *abbreviation* of a word w, we mean any word obtained from w by deleting some (possibly all or none) occurrences of letters in w. For a language L, denote by *abbr* (L) the collection of all abbreviations of words in L. Prove that if L is regular, then so is also *abbr* (L) but that the converse of this statement is not true.

3. Show that every infinite regular language L such that $L \subseteq \{a\}^*$ and $\lambda \in L$ possesses FPP.

4. A finite deterministic automaton is a *permutation automaton* if it has no two distinct nodes q_1 and q_2 such that there is an arrow labeled by the same letter a both from q_1 and q_2 to a state q_3. Show by a direct argument that a language represented by a permutation automaton and containing the empty word possesses FPP. Determine also an upper bound in terms of the number of nodes for the order of the language. (Cf. [Li1].)

5. A language L is a *star language* if $L = L_1^*$, for some language L_1, referred to as a *root* of L. A root of L is *minimal* if it is contained in every root of L. Show that if a nonempty regular language L_1 is a minimal root, then $L_1 \cup \{\lambda\}$ does not possess FPP. (Cf. [Li1].)

6. Assume that α, β, and γ are words such that $\alpha\beta^i\gamma$ is in R^* for every $i \geq 0$. Show that there are integers m, n, and p such that the words

$$x = \alpha\beta^m, y = \beta^n, z = \beta^p\gamma$$

satisfy (3.19).

7. Formulate and prove the converse of Lemma 3.10. (Cf. also the proof of Theorem 3.15.)

Chapter 4

CODES AND EQUALITY SETS

4.1 CHARACTERISTIC PROPERTIES OF CODES

The purpose of this chapter is two-fold. In the first place, we want to make a brief excursion into the theory of codes. This theory has produced a number of beautiful results applicable to various parts of language theory. In the second place, we want to discuss some closely related notions introduced very recently. These notions will be needed in Chapters 5 and 6.

We want to emphasize that we shall not discuss so-called error-correcting codes. We shall be concerned exclusively with algebraic code theory, usually regarded as a part of semigroup theory.

Intuitively, a code is a set of words such that any product of these words can be "decoded" in a unique fashion. For instance, consider the set of words

$$\{a, bb, aab, bab\}. \tag{4.1}$$

These words can be used to encode the letters 0, 1, 2, 3; and this encoding can be extended "morphically" to an encoding of the words over the alphabet $\{0, 1, 2, 3\}$. Thus, the word 012230 will be encoded as *abbaabaabbaba*. That the decoding will never lead to ambiguities is guaranteed by the fact that every word over the alphabet $\{a, b\}$ can be factorized in at most one way as a product of the words (4.1). This fact is easy to establish if one reads words over $\{a, b\}$ from right to left: every encoded word must end with exactly one of the words (4.1). In this way the letters 0, 1, 2, 3 are found out one by one from the right end. This means that (4.1) is a code.

On the other hand, the set $\{a, ab, ba\}$ is not a code. For instance, the word *aba* can be decoded in two different ways:

$$aba = (ab)a = a(ba).$$

55

Definition. A nonempty language C over an alphabet Σ is a *code* if, whenever

$$x_{i_1}, \ldots, x_{i_m}, x_{j_1}, \ldots, x_{j_n}$$

are in C and satisfy

$$x_{i_1} \cdots x_{i_m} = x_{j_1} \cdots x_{j_n}, \tag{4.2}$$

then $x_{i_1} = x_{j_1}$. $\square$

Clearly, if C is a code then (4.2) implies that $m = n$ and $x_{i_t} = x_{j_t}$, for $t = 1, \ldots, m$. Thus, every word in C^* can be decoded in a unique fashion as a product of words in C. It is also clear that the empty word can never be contained in a code and that a nonempty subset of a code is itself a code. We assume that the alphabet Σ contains at least two letters because one-letter alphabets are trivial as regards codes. We prove now two fairly simple characterization results for codes.

Lemma 4.1. A nonempty language C over an alphabet Σ is a code if and only if there is a set of symbols Σ_1 and a bijection of Σ_1 onto C which can be extended to an injective morphism of Σ_1^* into Σ^*.

Proof. Observe first that Σ_1 may be an infinite set of symbols; the meaning of Σ_1^* should still be clear.

Consider the "if" part. Assume that Σ_1 and a bijection $\varphi : \Sigma_1 \to C$ satisfying the condition concerning extension exist. To prove that C is a code, we consider arbitrary words $x_{i_1}, \ldots, x_{i_m}, x_{j_1}, \ldots, x_{j_n}$ in C satisfying (4.2). Denoting $\varphi^{-1}(x_{i_t}) = a_{i_t}$ (resp. $\varphi^{-1}(x_{j_t}) = a_{j_t}$), we obtain

$$\varphi(a_{i_1} \cdots a_{i_m}) = x_{i_1} \cdots x_{i_m} = x_{j_1} \cdots x_{j_n} = \varphi(a_{j_1} \cdots a_{j_n}).$$

(We are now already considering the extension of φ into Σ_1^*.) But the fact that φ is injective implies that

$$a_{i_1} \cdots a_{i_m} = a_{j_1} \cdots a_{j_n}.$$

Consequently, $a_{i_1} = a_{j_1}$, whence

$$x_{i_1} = \varphi(a_{i_1}) = \varphi(a_{j_1}) = x_{j_1},$$

implying that C is a code.

Consider the "only if" part. Assume that C is a code. Let Σ_1 be a set of symbols of the same cardinality as C. Let $\varphi : \Sigma_1 \to C$ be a bijection, where the corresponding elements are denoted by the same lower indices. The mapping is extended to a morphism of $\Sigma_1{}^*$ into Σ^* in the natural way. We still have to prove that this extension of φ is injective.

Assume the contrary: there are elements of Σ_1 satisfying

$$\varphi(a_{i_1} \cdots a_{i_m}) = \varphi(a_{j_1} \cdots a_{j_n}), \; a_{i_1} \cdots a_{i_m} \neq a_{j_1} \cdots a_{j_n}. \tag{4.3}$$

We assume without loss of generality that m in (4.3) is smallest: (4.3) is not satisfied for any $m_1 < m$. Consequently, $a_{i_1} \neq a_{j_1}$. (For if $a_{i_1} = a_{j_1}$, we would obtain

$$\varphi(a_{i_2} \cdots a_{i_m}) = \varphi(a_{j_2} \cdots a_{j_n}), \; a_{i_2} \cdots a_{i_m} \neq a_{j_2} \cdots a_{j_n},$$

contradicting the minimality of m.) Thus, we have obtained

$$\varphi(a_{i_1} \cdots a_{i_m}) = x_{i_1} \cdots x_{i_m} = \varphi(a_{j_1} \cdots a_{j_n}) = x_{j_1} \cdots x_{j_n} \tag{4.4}$$

and $a_{i_1} \neq a_{j_1}$. But because φ is a bijection, the latter inequality implies $x_{i_1} \neq x_{j_1}$. This together with (4.4) contradicts the fact that C is a code. This result shows that the extended φ is injective. $\quad\square$

The following result is usually known as Schützenberger's criterion. We say that a language L is *catenatively independent* if no word w in L can be expressed as a product

$$w = w_1 \cdots w_n, \, n \geq 2, \, \text{each } w_i \text{ in } L.$$

Lemma 4.2. A catenatively independent nonempty language C over Σ is a code if and only if, whenever w is a word over Σ such that both C^*w and wC^* intersect C^*, then w is in C^*.

Proof. Consider again first the "if" part. Assuming that C satisfies the condition in the statement of the lemma, we have to show that C is a code. Assume the contrary: there are elements x_v of C satisfying

$$x_{i_1} \cdots x_{i_m} = x_{j_1} \cdots x_{j_n} \text{ and } x_{i_1} \neq x_{j_1}. \tag{4.5}$$

By (4.5), one of the words x_{i_1} and x_{j_1} is a proper prefix of the other. Without loss of generality we assume that

$$x_{j_1} = x_{i_1} y. \tag{4.6}$$

By (4.5) and (4.6), C^*y and C^* (resp. yC^* and C^*) intersect, the common element being x_{j_1} (resp. $x_{i_2} \cdots x_{i_m}$). (Observe that (4.5) and (4.6) imply that $m \geq 2$.) Because C satisfies the condition concerning intersections, we conclude that y is in C^*. By (4.6), this conclusion contradicts the assumption that C is catenatively independent.

Consider the "only if" part. We assume that C is a code and show indirectly that the condition concerning intersections is satisfied. Hence, assume this situation is not the case, i.e., there are elements x_ν of C, y_ν of C^* and $w \notin C^*$ such that

$$x_{i_1} \cdots x_{i_m} w = x_{j_1} \cdots x_{j_n} \text{ and } wy_1 = y_2. \tag{4.7}$$

Assuming again that m is minimal, we conclude that $x_{i_1} \neq x_{j_1}$. (Otherwise, we would obtain the situation (4.7) with a smaller value of m.) We obtain now

$$\begin{aligned} x_{i_1} \cdots x_{i_m} wy_1 &= x_{j_1} \cdots x_{j_n} y_1 \\ &= x_{i_1} \cdots x_{i_m} y_2, x_{i_1} \neq x_{j_1}, \end{aligned}$$

contradicting the fact that C is a code.   □

The condition of Lemma 4.2 can be stated also in the following more compact form: for every w in Σ^*,

$$C^*w \cap wC^* \cap C^* \neq \phi \text{ implies } w \in C^*. \tag{4.8}$$

Clearly, if the three sets C^*w, wC^* and C^* intersect, then also C^*w and C^*, as well as wC^* and C^*, intersect. Conversely, if

$$wx_1 = x_2 \quad \text{and} \quad x_3w = x_4, \quad \text{where} \quad x_1, x_2, x_3, x_4 \in C^*,$$

then $wx_1x_4 = x_2x_4 = x_2x_3w$, showing that all three sets intersect. Observe, however, that condition (4.8) alone (without the assumption of C being catenatively independent) does not guarantee that C is a code.

The characterizations of Lemmas 4.1 and 4.2 do not directly give an effective method for testing whether or not a given language is a code. Various algorithms are known for testing whether or not a given finite language is a code. In fact, the results of Chapter 2 immediately yield the following algorithm: one checks whether or not $x_1C^* \cap x_2C^*$ is empty for every pair

(x_1, x_2) of distinct elements of C. The algorithm resulting from the following theorem is the oldest and is originally due to Sardinas and Patterson, [SarP].

Theorem 4.3. Assume that C is a nonempty language over Σ. Define inductively the languages $C_0, C_1, C_2, \ldots$ over Σ as follows:

$$C_0 = C,$$

$$C_{i+1} = \{w \in \Sigma^+ \mid yw = x \text{ or } xw = y, \text{ for some } x \in C, y \in C_i\}.$$

Then C is a code if and only if $C_i \cap C = \phi$, for every $i \geq 1$.

Before proving the theorem, we note that if C is finite then every word in every C_i is of length at most equal to the length of the longest word in C. Hence, there can be at most finitely many distinct languages C_i, and we obtain indeed an algorithm for deciding whether or not C is a code. (Cf. also Exercise 1.) For instance, choose C to be the set (4.1). In this case,

$$C_1 = \{ab\}, C_2 = \{b\}, C_3 = \{b, ab\} = C_4 = C_5 \ldots .$$

Because $C_i \cap C = \phi$, for every $i \geq 1$, we infer that C is a code. On the other hand, considering

$$C = \{a, ab, ba\},$$

we obtain $C_1 = \{b\}, C_2 = \{a\}$. Because $C_2 \cap C \neq \phi$, C is not a code.

Proof. Consider first the "if" part. We show that if C is not a code, then one of the sets C_i intersects C.

Because C is not a code, there are elements x_v of C satisfying (4.5). The situation can be depicted as follows:

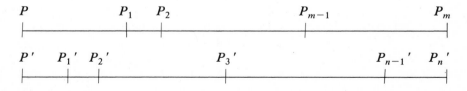

The idea is that $x_{i_1} \cdots x_{i_m}$ is written on the upper line: the segment from P to P_1 contains x_{i_1}, the segment from P_1 to P_2 contains x_{i_2}, and so forth. Similarly, the word $x_{j_1} \cdots x_{j_n}$ is written on the lower line. Because $x_{i_1} \neq x_{j_1}$, the points P_1 and $P_1{}'$ are not on the same vertical line. (In the picture it is assumed that x_{j_1} is a proper prefix of x_{i_1}.) Assuming again the minimality of m in (4.5), we may conclude that none of the primed points, apart from the first and the last, is on the same vertical line with a non-primed point.

Recall that the words in C_{i+1} are obtained either by erasing a prefix belonging to C_i from a word in C, or else by erasing a prefix belonging to C from a word in C_i. Thus, in our picture, the word in the segment $P_1{}'P_1$ is in C_1, the word in the segment $P_2{}'P_1$ in C_2, the word in the segment $P_1P_3{}'$ in C_3, and the word in the segment $P_2P_3{}'$ in C_4. Continuing in this way, we conclude that either x_{j_n} is in one of the sets C_i (this happens in the situation depicted above), or else that x_{i_m} is in one of the sets C_i (this happens if P_{m-1} is closer to the common end point than $P_{n-1}{}'$). In any case, one of the sets C_i intersects C.

Consider then the "only if" part. Assume that C is a code. We claim first that

$$C^*w \cap C^* \neq \phi \text{ for all } w \in C_i, \text{ whenever } i \geq 0. \qquad (4.9)$$

Indeed, for $i = 0$, (4.9) is obvious. (Recall that $C_0 = C$.) Assume inductively (4.9) for the value $i - 1$, and consider $w \in C_i, i \geq 1$. By the definition of C_i, there are $x \in C$ and $y \in C_{i-1}$ such that

$$xw = y \quad \text{or} \quad yw = x. \qquad (4.10)$$

By the inductive hypothesis,

$$x_1 y = x_2,$$

for some x_1 and x_2 in C^*. Consequently, either

$$x_1 xw = x_1 y = x_2 \quad \text{or} \quad x_1 yw = x_2 w = x_1 x,$$

depending on which of the alternatives (4.10) is satisfied. In both cases we see that $C^*w \cap C^* \neq \phi$, completing the proof of (4.9).

To show that C does not intersect any of the sets $C_i, i \geq 1$, we assume the contrary:

$$C \cap C_i \neq \phi \quad \text{for some} \quad i \geq 1.$$

Consequently, by definition of C_i, there are

$$x \in C, x' \in C, \quad \text{and} \quad y \in C_{i-1}$$

such that either

$$yx = x' \quad \text{or} \quad x'x = y. \tag{4.11}$$

Consider the first alternative. Then (4.9) implies that

$$yC^* \cap C^* \neq \phi \quad \text{and} \quad C^*y \cap C^* \neq \phi,$$

which gives by Lemma 4.2 the result $y \in C^*$. However, this conclusion is impossible because $yx = x'$ and C is a code.

Hence, the second alternative in (4.11) must hold. This result implies that $i \geq 2$ because, otherwise, y would be an element of C expressed as a product of two elements of C. Consequently, there are $y_1 \in C_{i-2}$ and $x'' \in C$ such that either

$$y_1y = x'' \quad \text{or} \quad x''y = y_1.$$

The first alternative is ruled out as above by the equation $y_1x'x = x''$, by (4.9) and by Lemma 4.2. Hence, the second alternative must hold:

$$x''y = x''x'x = y_1.$$

If $i = 2$, this fact implies that an element of C can be written as the product of three elements of C. Consequently, we must have $i \geq 3$.

Continuing in the same fashion, we see that i must be greater than any preassigned integer. Hence, we conclude that $C \cap C_i = \phi$ for all i.   □

4.2   MAXIMAL CODES

A code C over an alphabet Σ is *maximal* if, for all codes $C' \supseteq C$ over Σ, we have $C' = C$. For instance, the code

$$C = \{aa, ab, ba, bb\}$$

is maximal. Clearly, if w is a word over $\{a, b\}$ and $w \notin C$, then $C \cup \{w\}$ is not a code. This conclusion follows because w^2 can be factorized in two different ways.

Maximal codes can be characterized by means of a certain numerical quantity associated with languages. This is a very rare phenomenon in language theory: a class of languages is characterized by means of a numerical quantity.

The *code indicator* of a word w over an alphabet Σ with $n \geq 2$ letters is defined by

$$ci(w) = n^{-|w|}.$$

Let L be a language over Σ, where Σ has $n \geq 2$ letters. (We assume Σ is the minimal alphabet of L, i.e., L is not a language over any proper subset of Σ.) Then the *code indicator* of L, in symbols $ci(L)$, is defined to be the sum of the code indicators of all words in L. Thus, if L is finite then $ci(L)$ is a positive rational. If L is infinite, $ci(L)$ is either a positive real (in case the series converges), or is equal to infinity.

For instance, if L is the language (4.1), we obtain

$$ci(L) = \frac{1}{2} + \frac{1}{4} + \frac{1}{8} + \frac{1}{8} = 1.$$

By imposing an upper bound for the code indicator, we are able to capture the intuitive ideas first that a code should not have too many words, and second that short words rather than long words increase the likelihood of a language not being a code. This leads to the following theorem.

Theorem 4.4.   Every code C satisfies $ci(C) \leq 1$.

Proof.   Assume first that C is a finite code over an alphabet with $n \geq 2$ letters. Following the definition of a code, it is easy to verify that every power C^j, $j \geq 1$, is also a code.

We show now by induction on j that

$$ci(C^j) = (ci(C))^j, \quad \text{for all } j \geq 1. \tag{4.12}$$

This is trivially true for $j = 1$. Assuming inductively (4.12) for a fixed value j, we consider the power C^{j+1}. Because C^{j+1} is a code, each of its words can be represented uniquely in the form xw, where $x \in C$ and $w \in C^j$. Assuming C consists of the words $x_1, \ldots, x_t$ and denoting

$$c_\alpha = n^{-|x_\alpha|}, \text{ for } \alpha = 1, \ldots, t,$$

we obtain

$$ci(C^{j+1}) = \sum_{\alpha=1}^{t} c_\alpha ci(C^j) = ci(C^j) \sum_{\alpha=1}^{t} c_\alpha$$

$$= (ci(C))^j ci(C) = (ci(C))^{j+1}.$$

(Here the inductive assumption and the equation $ci(w_1 w_2) = ci(w_1)ci(w_2)$ have been used.) Consequently, (4.12) is valid.

If the length of the longest (resp. shortest) word in C is K (resp. k), then every word in C^j is of length $\geq kj$ and $\leq Kj$. Consequently, there are at most $(K - k)j + 1$ different lengths possible among the words of C^j. On the other hand, $ci(L) \leq 1$ for any language L such that all words in L are of the same length. These observations give us the estimate

$$ci(C^j) \leq (K - k)j + 1.$$

Applying (4.12), we obtain

$$(ci(C))^j \leq (K - k)j + 1,$$

for all j. Because $K - k$ is independent of j, this state is possible only if $ci(C) \leq 1$.

The result can now readily be extended to the case where C is infinite. Clearly, C must be denumerable:

$$C = \{x_1, x_2, \ldots\}.$$

If $ci(C) > 1$, there is a finite subset

$$C' = \{x_1, x_2, \ldots, x_t\}$$

of C satisfying $ci(C') > 1$. The fact that a subset of a code is always a code would contradict the first part of the proof.   □

The following result is now an immediate corollary of Theorem 4.4 and the definition of a code indicator.

Theorem 4.5.   A code C satisfying the condition $ci(C) = 1$ is maximal.

The next theorem shows that, for finite codes, the converse of Theorem 4.5 holds as well.

Theorem 4.6.   A finite code C is maximal if and only if $ci(C) = 1$.

Proof.   By Theorem 4.5, it suffices to show that a finite maximal code C satisfies the condition $ci(C) = 1$. Assume again that C is over the alphabet Σ with cardinality $n \geq 2$ and that the length of the longest (resp. shortest) word in C equals K (resp. k).

Since C is a finite maximal code, a word $y \in C^*$ has the following property: for every $x \in \Sigma^*$, there is $x' \in \Sigma^*$ such that $yxx' \in C^*$. (Cf. Exercise 4.) We let p be a sufficiently large integer and let x range through Σ^p. Then each of the words

$$z(x) = yxx' \tag{4.13}$$

is of length $\geq |y| + p$ and $\leq |y| + p + K$. (x' can be chosen such that $|x'| < K$.) Hence, there are positive numbers q_1 and q_2 independent of p such that each of the words (4.13) (when x ranges through Σ^p) is in some language C^j, where

$$q_1 p \leq j \leq q_2 p.$$

Since the range of j is linear with respect to p and since the number of the words (4.13) equals n^p, there is a positive number q_3 independent of p such that some C^{j_0} contains at least $q_3 n^p / p$ of the words (4.13).

Assume now that $ci(C) < 1$. We apply the relation (4.12), obtaining

$$(ci(C))^{q_1 p} \geq (ci(C))^{j_0} = ci(C^{j_0})$$
$$\geq (q_3 n^p / p) n^{-(|y| + p + K)}.$$

(Recall that the words (4.13) are of length $\leq |y| + p + K$.) But this situation means that there is a positive number q_4 independent of p such that

$$(ci(C))^{q_1 p} \geq q_4 / p$$

holds for all (sufficiently large) p. This condition is possible only if $ci(C) \geq 1$, a contradiction.

By Theorem 4.4 we conclude that $ci(C) = 1$. $\square$

4.3   CODES WITH BOUNDED DELAY

Of the special classes of codes investigated in the literature, codes with bounded delay are of interest from the point of view of many problems in language theory, in particular, the DOL equivalence problem considered in the next chapter. Before giving the definition, we consider as an example the code

$$C = \{a, ab, bb\}.$$

Suppose one has to decode a word of the form ab^i, reading the word from left to right. Then one has to read through the whole word before decoding it because the first decoded letter depends on the parity of the number of b's. Such a situation is not possible if the given code has bounded delay from left to right: in this case always a certain fixed amount of look-ahead is sufficient. An extreme example is provided by codes like

$$C_1 = \{aa, ab, ba\},$$

where no look-ahead is needed for decoding. This fact is true also with respect to the code C if one decodes words from right to left!

Definition.   A code C has *bounded delay $p \geq 1$ from left to right* if, whenever

$$x_{i_1} \cdots x_{i_p} \text{ is a prefix of } x_{j_1} \cdots x_{j_n} \tag{4.14}$$

where the x's are words of C, then $x_{i_1} = x_{j_1}$. Bounded delay from *right to left* is defined analogously, using suffixes. A code C has *bounded delay* from left to right (resp. from right to left, or in both directions) if there is a p such that C has bounded delay p from left to right (resp. from right to left, or in both directions).

Thus, considering the examples above, both C and C_1 have bounded delay 1 from right to left (codes with this property are referred to as *suffix codes*), and C_1 has also bounded delay 1 from left to right (codes with this property are referred to as *prefix codes*). The code C has no bounded delay from left to right.

If a code has bounded delay p, it also has bounded delay p_1, for any $p_1 \geq p$. Observe also that the condition defining the notion of bounded delay is satisfied only by codes. Thus, we could say equivalently in the definition: "A language C is a code of bounded delay p. ...."

Clearly, a code C is a prefix code (resp. a suffix code) if and only if there are no nonempty words x and y such that both x and xy (resp. x and yx) are in C. Codes that are both prefix and suffix codes are referred to as *biprefix codes*.

The following simple lemma gives a property of bounded delay codes used quite often to define them. We state the lemma for the direction from left to right. The analogous statement holds for the other direction.

Lemma 4.7.   A code C over the alphabet Σ has bounded delay p from left to right if and only if, for all $x \in C^*$, $y \in C^{p-1}$, and $w \in \Sigma^*$,

$$xyw \in C^* \text{ implies } yw \in C^*. \tag{4.15}$$

Proof.   Assume that C is of bounded delay p from left to right and consider $xyw \in C^*$ as in (4.15). If $x = \lambda$, (4.15) holds. Assume $x \in C^+$. Then we may write

$$xy = x_{i_1} \cdots x_{i_q}, q \geq p, xyw = x_{j_1} \cdots x_{j_n}.$$

Because xy is a prefix of xyw, we obtain $x_{i_1} = x_{j_1}$. Consequently, if the prefix x_{i_1} is deleted from xyw, we still obtain a word in C^*. Continuing such deletions in the same way, we conclude that $yw \in C^*$.

Assume, conversely, that (4.15) is satisfied. Assume that (4.14) holds for some x's in C. Hence,

$$x_{j_1} \cdots x_{j_n} = x_{i_1} \cdots x_{i_p} w,$$

for some $w \in \Sigma^*$. Choosing in (4.15)

$$x = x_{i_1} \quad \text{and} \quad y = x_{i_2} \cdots x_{i_p},$$

we infer that the word obtained from $x_{j_1} \cdots x_{j_n}$ by deleting the prefix x_{i_1} is in C^*, i.e.,

$$x_{j_1} \cdots x_{j_n} = x_{i_1} y_1 \text{ where } y_1 \in C^*.$$

The fact that C is a code implies that $x_{j_1} = x_{i_1}$, showing that C has bounded delay p from left to right. $\square$

We now introduce the notion of a *composition* of two codes. For this purpose it is useful to identify codes with certain morphisms. We say that a morphism $h : \Sigma_1^* \to \Sigma^*$ is a *code* if the language

$$\{h(a) \mid a \in \Sigma_1\}$$

is a code. (Here Σ is an alphabet, and Σ_1 is an alphabet or an infinite set of symbols.) Clearly, every code can be viewed as a morphism in this sense, i.e., as an injective morphism, cf. Lemma 4.1. The *composition* of two codes is simply the composition of the corresponding morphisms (provided the latter composition exists).

The cardinality of the first code must equal the cardinality of the alphabet of the second code for the composition to exist. If this is the case, the composition still depends on the choice of the bijection involved in case the codes are given as languages rather than as morphisms. For instance,

$$\{a,\ aba,\ baba,\ bb,\ bbba\}$$

is the composition of the two codes

$$\{a,\ ba,\ bb\} \quad \text{and} \quad \{0,\ 01,\ 11,\ 2,\ 21\},$$

obtained from the bijection $\varphi(0) = a$, $\varphi(1) = ba$, $\varphi(2) = bb$.

Because injectivity is preserved in compositions, it is clear that the composition of two codes is indeed again a code. The following result will be needed later on in connection with elementary morphisms.

Lemma 4.8.   The composition of two codes with bounded delay from left to right (resp. from right to left) is a code with bounded delay from left to right (resp. from right to left).

Proof.   Let C_i have bounded delay p_i from left to right, for $i = 1, 2$. We claim that the composition of C_1 and C_2 is of bounded delay $p_1 + p_2 - 1$.

Assume that C_i is defined by the morphism h_i, for $i = 1, 2$, and that

$$h_1(h_2(au)) \text{ is a prefix of } h_1(h_2(bv)), \tag{4.16}$$

where a and b are letters, and u and v are words such that

$$|u| = (p_1 + p_2 - 1) - 1.$$

We have to show that $a = b$.

Write u in the form $u = u_2 u_1$, where

$$|u_i| = p_i - 1, \text{ for } i = 1, 2. \tag{4.17}$$

Denote

$$h_2(au_2) = c_1 \cdots c_t, \, h_2(u_1) = c_{t+1} \cdots c_{t+t'},$$

where the c's are letters. By (4.17), $t' \geq p_1 - 1$. (Clearly h_1 and h_2 are nonerasing.) Denote further the first t letters of $h_2(bv)$ by $c_1', \ldots, c_t'$. (By (4.16), such letters must exist.) It suffices to show that

$$c_i = c_i', \text{ for } i = 1, \ldots, t, \tag{4.18}$$

because (4.18) implies that $h_2(au_2)$ is a prefix of $h_2(bv)$, whence $a = b$ because h_2 is of bounded delay p_2.

To prove (4.18), observe first that by (4.16)

$$h_1(c_1 \cdots c_{t+t'}) \text{ is a prefix of } h_1(h_2(bv)),$$

whence $c_1 = c_1'$ because h_1 is of bounded delay p_1 and $t + t' - 1 \geq t' \geq p_1 - 1$. Considering now the word $c_2 \cdots c_{t+t'}$ and the word obtained from $h_2(bv)$ by deleting the first letter $c_1' = c_1$, we conclude in the same way that $c_2 = c_2'$. This procedure can be continued, and because $t' \geq p_1 - 1$, we obtain also $c_t = c_t'$.

The proof of Lemma 4.8 in case of bounded delay from right to left is carried out exactly as above.   □

4.4   EQUALITY SETS AND THEIR REGULARITY

Given two morphisms g and h mapping Σ^* into Σ_1^* (where Σ and Σ_1 are alphabets and possibly $\Sigma_1 = \Sigma$), we define their *equality language* or *equality set* by

$$E(g, h) = \{w \in \Sigma^* \, | \, g(w) = h(w)\}.$$

For instance, if g and h are defined on $\{a, b\}^*$ by

$$g(a) = h(b) = a, \, g(b) = h(a) = aa,$$

then $E(g, h)$ consists of all words w such that the number of occurrences of a in w equals that of b in w. It is easy to see that in this case $E(g, h)$ is not regular.

For the morphisms g and h defined by

$$g(a) = aab, g(b) = a,$$
$$h(a) = a, h(b) = baa,$$

we have $E(g, h) = \{a^2b^2\}^*$. For the morphisms g and h defined by

$$g(a) = aab, g(b) = aa,$$
$$h(a) = a, h(b) = baa,$$

we have $E(g, h) = \{\lambda\}$. The verification of these results is left to the reader. Since λ is always in the equality set, we say in the sequel that the equality set is *empty* if it consists of λ only. Thus, in our last example above the equality set is empty.

Equality sets are often useful in language theory, as will also be seen in Chapters 5 and 6. As regards decidability results, it is a "desirable" situation that the equality sets considered are regular. Our first example above shows that this condition is not true in general. Our following theorem shows that this condition is true for a certain class of morphisms. The theorem is of crucial importance in the solution of the DOL equivalence problem.

Theorem 4.9. Assume that the morphisms g and h are finite codes with bounded delay in the same direction. Then $E(g, h)$ is regular.

Before proving Theorem 4.9, we introduce an auxiliary notion that is also of interest on its own right. We say that a pair (g, h) of morphisms possesses the *property of unique continuation* if there is a constant k such that the following condition is satisfied. Whenever x is a prefix of $w \in E(g, h)$ and

$$||g(x)| - |h(x)|| > k, \tag{4.19}$$

then there is a unique letter a such that xa is a prefix of a word in $E(g, h)$.

A special case of the property of unique continuation is the situation where there is a constant k such that (4.19) never holds for prefixes of words in $E(g, h)$. In this case we say that the pair (g, h) has *bounded balance*, cf. also Exercise 8. Of the three examples considered above, the last two pairs (g, h) have indeed bounded balance, whereas the first pair does not even have the property of unique continuation.

Lemma 4.10. Each pair (g, h) of finite codes with bounded delay in the same direction possesses the property of unique continuation.

Proof.   We assume that g and h have bounded delay from left to right, the proof being analogous for the case of bounded delay from right to left. Let p be the maximum of the two delays. Let q be the maximum of the lengths $|g(a)|$ and $|h(a)|$, where a ranges through the domain alphabets of g and h. (Clearly, we may assume that the domain alphabet of g and h coincide.) We now choose $k = pq$ and claim that this k satisfies the condition in the definition of the property of unique continuation.

Indeed, assume (4.19) holds for a prefix x of a word in $E(g, h)$. This supposition implies that

$$g(x) = h(x)u \text{ or } h(x) = g(x)u, \text{ with } |u| > k.$$

We assume that the former alternative holds. We now make use of the fact that h is of bounded delay p. (In case of the latter alternative we similarly use the fact that g is of bounded delay p.) Assume that there are distinct letters a_1 and a_2 such that both xa_1 and xa_2 appear as prefixes of words in $E(g, h)$. Because of the equation $g(x) = h(x)u$, this implies that there are words y_1 and y_2 such that u is a prefix of both $h(a_1y_1)$ and $h(a_2y_2)$. Because $|u| > pq$, we conclude that $|y_1| \geq p$ and that there is a prefix $y_1{}'$ of y_1 such that $|y_1{}'|$ $= p - 1$ and $h(a_1y_1{}')$ is a prefix of u. Hence, $h(a_1y_1{}')$ is also a prefix of $h(a_2y_2)$. Because $a_1 \neq a_2$, this statement contradicts the fact that h is of bounded delay p from left to right.   □

Proof of Theorem 4.9.   We assume without loss of generality that g and h have bounded delay from left to right and that they have common domain and range alphabets Σ and Σ_1. By Lemma 4.10, the pair (g, h) possesses the property of unique continuation. Let k be the constant involved, cf. (4.19).

We can now show by the following argument that a finite deterministic automaton A represents the language $E(g, h)$. (Observe that we shall only show the existence of such an automation. Indeed, it is known that the construction cannot be carried out effectively.)

The automaton A has a "buffer" of length k. When reading an input word, A remembers which of the two morphisms "runs faster" and also the excessive part of the image up to the length of the buffer. An input x is immediately rejected if, for some prefix x_1 of x, neither one of the words $g(x_1)$ and $h(x_1)$ is a prefix of the other. In case of an overflow of the buffer, i.e., if one of the morphisms runs so much faster that the excessive part of the image is longer than k, we make use of the unique continuation property: there is at most one sequence of letters

$$a_1, a_2, \ldots, a_t \tag{4.20}$$

leading back to a k-bounded buffer, i.e., to a situation where the excessive part of the image is of length $\leq k$.

More formally, the automaton A has a node s which is both the initial and the only final node, and a "garbage" node r which can never be left once it is entered. It has also nodes labeled by (w, g) and (w, h), where w is a nonempty word over Σ_1 with length $\leq k$. (The node (w, g) contains the information that the word x read so far satisfies $g(x) = h(x)w$.) Moreover, A possesses a sequence of $t - 1$ nodes for each of the (finitely many) sequences (4.20).

Typical transitions are the following. If $g(a) = h(a)w$ and $|w| \leq k$ then there is an arrow labeled by a from s to (w, g). If $h(a) = wg(a)$, there is an arrow labeled by a from (w, g) to s. If $wg(a) = h(a)w_1$ and $|w_1| \leq k$, there is an arrow labeled by a from (w, g) to (w_1, g). If $h(a)$ is not a prefix of $wg(a)$, there is an arrow labeled by a from (w, g) to r. If $wg(a) = h(a)w_1$ and $|w_1| > k$, there is an arrow labeled by a from (w, g) to the first node in the sequence of nodes determined by the corresponding sequence (4.20). (Observe that this sequence depends only on the pair (w_1, g), i.e., only on the information concerning which of the morphisms runs faster and what the excessive part of the image is. We can give no effective bound on the length of this sequence; this is the reason why the construction of A is not effective.)

The reader should now have no difficulties in completing the definition of A and showing that A represents $E(g, h)$. $\square$

The following modification of Theorem 4.9 will not be needed in our subsequent considerations.

Theorem 4.11.   Assume that g is an arbitrary morphism and h a finite code with bounded delay in both directions. Then $E(g, h)$ is regular.

Proof.   The only difference with respect to the previous proof is that we have to show that the pair (g, h) now also has the property of unique continuation. In situations where g "runs faster," i.e., $g(x) = h(x)u$ we argue exactly as in the proof of Lemma 4.10, applying the fact that h has bounded delay from left to right. Consider a situation where h runs faster, i.e., $h(x) = g(x)u$ where u is long. Let xay (where a is a letter) be a word in $E(g, h)$. Then $g(y) = vh(y)$ where v is long. From this the uniqueness of a now follows, by applying the fact that h has bounded delay from right to left. $\square$

Theorems 4.9 and 4.11 cannot be further strengthened to concern the case where g and h have bounded delay in different directions, cf. Exercise 9.

4.5   ELEMENTARY MORPHISMS

A morphism $h : \Sigma^* \to \Sigma_1^*$ (where Σ and Σ_1 are alphabets, and possibly $\Sigma = \Sigma_1$) is *simplifiable* if there is an alphabet Σ_2 with a cardinality smaller than that of Σ and morphisms

$$f : \Sigma^* \to \Sigma_2^* \quad \text{and} \quad g : \Sigma_2^* \to \Sigma_1^*$$

such h equals the composition of gf. Otherwise, h is called *elementary*.

We shall make use of elementary morphisms in the solution of the DOL equivalence problem in Chapter 5. It is easy to see that an elementary morphism is always nonerasing. The composition of two simplifiable morphisms is itself simplifiable, whereas the composition of two elementary morphisms need not be elementary. (Cf. also Exercise 10.)

The following theorem will be our most important tool concerning elementary morphisms.

Theorem 4.12.   Every elementary morphism is a code with bounded delay in both directions.

Proof.   We say that a morphism $h : \Sigma^* \to \Sigma^*$ is *atomic* if there are distinct letters a and b in Σ such that either

$$h(a) = ab, h(c) = c \text{ for all } c \neq a, \qquad (4.21)$$

or else

$$h(a) = ba, h(c) = c \text{ for all } c \neq a. \qquad (4.22)$$

If (4.21) holds, then clearly h is a prefix code. If (4.22) holds, then h is of bounded delay 2 from left to right. Arguing similarly from right to left, we conclude that atomic morphisms have bounded delay in both directions.

Now let $h : \Sigma^* \to \Sigma_1^*$ be elementary. We claim that there are an integer $t \geq 0$, atomic morphisms $g_i : \Sigma^* \to \Sigma^*$, $i = 1, \ldots, t$, and a biprefix code $f : \Sigma^* \to \Sigma_1^*$ such that

$$h = f g_1 \cdots g_t. \qquad (4.23)$$

From this claim Theorem 4.12 immediately follows, by Lemma 4.8.

The claim is established by induction on

$$S(h) = \sum_{a \text{ in } \Sigma} |h(a)|.$$

Since h is elementary and hence nonerasing, $S(h)$ is greater than or equal to the cardinality of Σ. If $S(h)$ equals the cardinality of Σ, then h itself is a biprefix code and, consequently, (4.23) holds with $t = 0$. (Clearly, h being elementary implies that, whenever a and b are distinct letters, then also $h(a)$ and $h(b)$ are distinct letters.) Thus, the basis of induction is clear.

As an inductive hypothesis, assume that our claim holds for $S(h) \le n$. Consider an arbitrary elementary morphism $h : \Sigma^* \to \Sigma_1^*$ with $S(h) = n + 1$. If h is a biprefix code, there is nothing to prove. So assume (without loss of generality) that h is not a prefix code. This assumption implies that there are distinct letters a and b and a word x such that

$$h(a) = h(b)x.$$

Consider the atomic morphism $g : \Sigma^* \to \Sigma^*$ defined by

$$g(a) = ba, g(c) = c \text{ for } c \ne a,$$

as well as the morphism $h' : \Sigma^* \to \Sigma_1^*$ defined by

$$h'(a) = x, h'(c) = h(c) \text{ for } c \ne a.$$

(If h is not a suffix code, then an atomic morphism of the form (4.21) has to be used.)

Clearly, $h = h'g$ and $S(h') \le n$. Moreover, h' must be elementary because, otherwise, h would be simplifiable. Consequently, by our inductive hypothesis, a decomposition of the form (4.23) is found for h. □

Observe that in the decomposition (4.23) f is, in fact, also elementary. Thus, every elementary morphism can be expressed as a decomposition fg, where f is an elementary biprefix code and g is a product of atomic morphisms. It can also be shown that conversely every decomposition of this form is elementary.

As a direct corollary of Theorems 4.9 and 4.12 we now obtain the following important result.

Theorem 4.13. If g and h are elementary morphisms, then $E(g, h)$ is regular.

If Theorem 4.11 is used instead of Theorem 4.9, we obtain by Theorem 4.12 the result that $E(g, h)$ is regular whenever one of g and h is elementary.

4.6   POST CORRESPONDENCE PROBLEM

We have already met various decidability results by exhibiting an effective procedure (an algorithm) that is capable of solving all instances of the problem under consideration. A typical example is the FPP problem considered in Chapter 3. Indeed, some of the most complicated results in this book are decidability results.

Decidability results can be based on the intuitive notion of an algorithm, whereas the notion of an algorithm has to be formalized in order to show that some problem is undecidable. The most common among such formalizations is a Turing machine, cf. [AHU] or [HU].

The customary way of establishing the undecidability of a certain problem P is to "reduce" P to a problem P_1 whose undecidability is known, by showing that if P is decidable then so is P_1. In language theory the most convenient among such problems P_1 is the *Post correspondence problem*: let $g : \Sigma^* \to \Sigma_1^*$ and $h : \Sigma^* \to \Sigma_1^*$ be morphisms and decide whether or not $E(g, h)$ is empty. The reader is referred to [Sa2] for a detailed discussion why the Post correspondence problem is undecidable.

Only the following brief intuitive argument will be given here.

We show first how any formalization of the intuitive notion of an algorithm leads to problems undecidable algorithmically. Consider any such formalization. The reader familiar with Turing machines, Markov normal algorithms or any other of the customary formalizations may choose his or her favorite one.

For any algorithm A and any input word x of A, there are two possibilities: either A *halts* with x, i.e., a terminating computation results when A is applied to x, or else A does not halt with x. In the latter case we say that A *loops* with x. The *halting problem* consists of deciding, for an arbitrary pair (A, x), whether A halts or loops with x.

A special case of the halting problem is the *self-applicability problem* defined as follows. A word $w(A)$ can be associated to every algorithm A, for instance, by writing all instructions of A one after the other, separated by markers. An algorithm A is termed *self-applicable* if A halts with $w(A)$. The *self-applicability problem* consists of deciding whether or not an arbitrary algorithm is self-applicable. Clearly, the self-applicability problem is a subproblem of the halting problem and, consequently, if the former is undecidable then so is the latter.

Assume that there is an algorithm A_0 for the self-applicability problem. Thus, A_0 halts with all inputs of the form $w(A)$ and produces the answer "yes" or "no," depending on whether or not A is self-applicable. We now modify A_0 by adding a nonterminating computation starting from the "yes"-answer. Thus, the resulting algorithm A_1 loops (resp. halts) with inputs of the form $w(A)$ where A is (resp. is not) self-applicable. We now run into a contradiction by considering the input $w(A_1)$. Consequently, the self-applicability problem is undecidable, and so is also the halting problem.

One can associate with each instance (A, x) of the halting problem a pair (g, h) of morphisms such that A halts with x if and only if $E(g, h)$ is non-empty. This is done by letting the pairs $(g(a), h(a))$ correspond to the instructions of A and by taking care that g simulates the computation of A "faster" than h, and that h "catches up" only at the end. (The reader is referred to the proof of Theorem 6.9 for an analogous construction.) One has to make sure that the definition of the pair (g, h) gives rise to no "parasite solutions," i.e., that $E(g, h)$ is nonempty only in case A halts with x. The association thus established shows the undecidability of the Post correspondence problem.

The undecidability of the Post correspondence problem means that no algorithm produces an answer for an arbitrary pair (g, h). Of course, there are particular pairs (g, h) for which the emptiness of $E(g, h)$ is easy to settle. On the other hand, the Post correspondence problem remains undecidable if attention is restricted to codes g and h, cf. [Le].

EXERCISES

1. Show that if $C_i = C_{i+1}$ (as defined in Theorem 4.3), then $C_i = C_{i+j}$ for all $j \geq 0$.

2. Show that if $C \subseteq \Sigma^*$ is a maximal code and $w \in \Sigma^*$, then $C^* \cap \Sigma^* w \Sigma^* \neq \phi$. (In semigroup terminology this means that C^* intersects all two-sided ideals of Σ^*.)

3. Show that the converse of Exercise 2 is not valid. ($C = \{a^{2 + |w|} bw \mid w \in \{a, b\}^*\}$ is a prefix code satisfying the condition, but it is not maximal.)

4. Show (using Exercise 2) that if $C \subseteq \Sigma^*$ is a finite maximal code, then there is $y \in C^*$ such that, for every $x \in \Sigma^*$, there is $x' \in \Sigma^*$ with the property $yxx' \in C^*$.

5. Assume that C is of bounded delay from left to right. Show that there is an integer t such that C^t is of bounded delay 2 from left to right.

6. Is the code $C = \{a, aba, baba, bb, bbba\}$ of bounded delay from left to right (resp. from right to left)? (Observe that C is the composition of a prefix code and a suffix code.)

7. Construct morphisms g and h satisfying, for given $m, n \geq 1$,

$$E(g, h) = \{a^m b^n\}*.$$

(Cf. [CuK].)

8. For $k \geq 0$, denote by $E_k(g, h)$ the subset of $E(g, h)$ consisting of all words w such that (4.19) holds for no prefix x of w. Show that $E_k(g, h)$ is regular, for any g, h and k. Show also that $E(g, h)$ is regular if and only if $E(g, h) = E_k(g, h)$, for some k. (Observe also that $E_k(g, h) \subseteq E_{k+1}(g, h)$, for all k, and that $E(g, h)$ equals the union of all sets $E_k(g, h)$.)

9. Consider the morphisms

$$g, h : \{a, b, c, d, e, f\}* \rightarrow \{1, 2, 3, 4, 5\}*$$

defined by the table

	a	b	c	d	e	f
g	1234	2323	4	24	32	5
h	1	23	4	42	3232	4325

Show that

$$E(g, h) = (\{abcb^2 \cdots cb^{2^n} de^{2^n} c \cdots e^2 cef \mid n \geq 0\} \cup \{c\})*.$$

Conclude that the equality set between a prefix code and a suffix code is not necessarily regular. (In fact, this particular $E(g, h)$ is not even a context-free language.) Cf. [KaS].

10. Consider the morphism h defined by

$$h(a) = de, \; h(b) = dfe, \; h(c) = dffe,$$
$$h(d) = a, \; h(e) = bc, \; h(f) = ba.$$

Prove that h is elementary, whereas h^2 is simplifiable. What is the smallest alphabet Σ for which you can give two elementary morphisms

$$g, h : \Sigma* \rightarrow \Sigma*$$

such that their product is simplifiable?

11. Assume that $\Sigma = \{a_1, \ldots, a_n\}$ and

$$h : \Sigma* \rightarrow \Sigma_1*$$

is elementary. Show that h is of bounded delay

$$|h(a_1 \cdots a_n)| - n + 1$$

from left to right, as well as from right to left. Show also that this estimate, as well as the estimate $p_1 + p_2 - 1$ obtained in the proof of Lemma 4.8 are the best possible ones in the general case.

12. A morphism $h: \Sigma^* \to \Sigma_1^*$ is called *periodic* if $h(\Sigma) \subseteq \{w\}^*$, for some word w. Show that the emptiness of $E(g, h)$ is decidable if one of g and h is periodic. (Cf. [KaS]. Apart from some trivialities and the situation of Exercise 13, this is the only case in which the Post correspondence problem is known to be decidable.)

13. Investigate the decidability of the Post correspondence problem in the case where the domain alphabets of g and h consist of two letters only. Cf. [CuK]. It has been shown recently (G. Rozenberg, personal communication) that the Post correspondence problem is decidable in this case. By the previous exercise, this result would follow directly from the decidability of the Post correspondence problem for elementary morphisms, which is still open.

Chapter 5

DECIDABLE AND UNDECIDABLE

5.1 OL SYSTEMS

This chapter deals with decidability questions. The difference between "decidable" and "undecidable" is illustrated within a specific language-theoretic framework: a problem is shown to be decidable for a certain class of languages, but if this class is made somewhat bigger, the same problem becomes undecidable.

In our considerations, "problems" consist of an infinity of instances, to each of which the answer is either "yes" or "no." A problem is *decidable* or *solvable* if there is an algorithm which for any instance of the problem outputs the answer to that instance. Otherwise, the problem is *undecidable* or *unsolvable.* As pointed out before, a formalization of the notion of an algorithm is necessary for establishing undecidability results. We do not give such a formalization. Our undecidability proofs consist of a reduction to the Post correspondence problem in the sense outlined at the end of Chapter 4.

Typical decidability problems considered in language theory are the following. Let M be a class of devices for defining languages. (Such an M might consist, for instance, of all grammars or automata of some type, or of all DOL systems.) By the *language equivalence* problem for M we understand the problem of determining of any two devices m_1 and m_2 whether or not they define the same language. In the *language inclusion* problem for M, one has to determine of arbitrary m_1 and m_2 in M whether or not the language defined by m_1 is included in the language defined by m_2. Clearly, a solution for the language inclusion problem yields a solution for the language equivalence problem. By the *emptiness* (resp. *finiteness*) problem for M we understand the problem of determining for an arbitrary device m in M whether or not the language defined by m is empty (resp. finite). The *membership* problem for M consists of deciding for an arbitrary m in M and for an arbitrary word w whether or not w belongs to the language defined by m.

For instance, Theorem 2.8 gives a solution of the language equivalence problem for finite automata (i.e., M is the class of finite automata).

It is clear that if a problem is decidable (resp. undecidable) for a class M, then so it is for any subset (resp. superset) of M. For decidability (resp. unde-cidability) results one usually tries to get M as large (resp. small) as possible to settle where the borderline between decidability and undecidability lies. In what follows, we shall see that deterministic and nondeterministic versions of the same class of devices yield decidable and undecidable language equiva-lence problems, respectively.

The notions of a DOL system and a DOL language were defined already in Chapter 1. DOL systems constitute the class of deterministic devices referred to above. Their nondeterministic counterpart, referred to as an OL system, will now be defined.

A mapping σ of an alphabet Σ into the set of finite subsets of Σ^* is termed a *finite substitution* (defined on Σ). The domain of σ is extended in the follow-ing fashion:

$$\sigma(\lambda) = \{\lambda\}, \; \sigma(w_1 w_2) = \sigma(w_1) \, \sigma(w_2),$$

for all w_1 and w_2 in Σ^*. (Juxtaposition on the right side stands for the catena-tion of languages.) Furthermore, for a language L over Σ, we define

$$\sigma(L) = \{u \,|\, u \in \sigma(w) \text{ for some } w \in L\}.$$

In what follows, we also iterate finite substitutions. Thus, σ^i stands for i consecutive applications of σ, where $i \geq 1$. By definition, $\sigma^0 (L) = L$.

Triples $G = (\Sigma, \sigma, w)$, where Σ is an alphabet, σ a finite substitution de-fined on Σ, and w a word over Σ, are referred to as *OL systems*. The language

$$L(G) = \bigcup_{i \geq 0} \sigma^i(w) \tag{5.1}$$

is referred to as the language defined or generated by the OL system G. Lan-guages of the form (5.1) are called *OL languages*.

For instance, the OL systems

$$G_1 = (\{a\}, \sigma_1, a^2) \quad \text{where} \quad \sigma_1(a) = \{a, a^2\},$$
$$G_2 = (\{a, b\}, \sigma_2, ab) \quad \text{where} \quad \sigma_2(a) = \{(ab)^2\}, \; \sigma_2(b) = \{\lambda\},$$
$$G_3 = (\{a, b\}, \sigma_3, a) \quad \text{where} \quad \sigma_3(a) = \sigma_3(b) = \{aa, ab, ba, bb\}$$

satisfy

$$L(G_1) = \{a^n | n \geq 2\},$$
$$L(G_2) = \{(ab)^{2^n} | n \geq 0\},$$
$$L(G_3) = \{a\} \cup \{w \in \{a, b\}^* | \text{ for some } n \geq 1, |w| = 2^n\}.$$

The finite substitution in an OL system can be viewed to specify a finite set of rewriting rules or productions. The notation is often chosen accordingly. Thus, we might introduce the above examples as follows:

$$G_1 = (\{a\}, \{a \to a, a \to a^2\}, a^2),$$
$$G_2 = (\{a, b\}, \{a \to (ab)^2, b \to \lambda\}, ab),$$
$$G_3 = (\{a, b\}, \{a \to aa, a \to ab, a \to ba, a \to bb, b \to aa, b \to ab,$$
$$b \to ba, b \to bb\}, a).$$

Observe, that G_2 is, in fact, a DOL system because σ_2 can be viewed as a morphism. This is always the case when $\sigma(a)$ consists of one word only, for all letters a.

If the finite substitution σ in an OL system G is viewed as defining a finite set of productions, then every word x in the language $L(G)$ is obtained from the axiom w by a derivation sequence

$$w = w_0, w_1, w_2, \ldots, w_n = x,$$

where each word is obtained from the preceding one by rewriting every letter according to some of the productions. In case of a DOL system this rewriting process is *deterministic*; the axiom determines the sequence uniquely if the length of the sequence is given. In fact, the letter "D" in "DOL" stands for "deterministic." DOL and OL systems are special types of *L systems*, where "L" comes from the name of Lindenmayer who first introduced such systems in 1968 as a model in developmental biology. Cf. [L]. The essential feature of L systems, as opposed to rewriting systems or phrase structure grammars defined in Chapter 2, is the *parallel* mode of the rewriting process: at each step of the process, every letter has to be rewritten. Finally, the letter "O" in "DOL" and "OL" indicates that rewriting happens in a context-free manner: the neighbors of a letter have no influence upon how the letter is rewritten. (Originally, "O" had a biological meaning to the effect that the communication between individual cells is zero-sided, i.e., there is no communication.)

It is easy to verify that the languages $L(G_1)$ and $L(G_3)$ given above are not at all DOL languages, i.e., the process in generating them is essentially non-deterministic.

The *language equivalence* problem for DOL (resp. OL) systems consists of determining of any two DOL (resp. OL) systems G and G' whether or not $L(G) = L(G')$. The word sequence $S(G)$ defined by a DOL system G was considered in Chapter 1. The *sequence equivalence* problem for DOL systems consists of determining of any two DOL systems G and G' whether or not $S(G) = S(G')$. (OL systems do not always generate a unique sequence of words. Hence, a sequence equivalence problem in the sense above does not exist for OL systems. Cf., however, Exercise 13.)

We shall see that sequence and language equivalence problems are decidable for DOL systems but that the language equivalence problem of OL systems is undecidable. Apart from exhibiting a typical borderline between decidability and undecidability, these results are also historically very interesting. The decidability status of DOL equivalence problems was open for quite a long time, and its solution brought about a number of new techniques and concepts, such as those of an elementary morphism and an equality set defined in the previous chapter. The study of the language equivalence problem of OL systems gave rise to some new ideas also concerning context-free languages.

5.2 DOL EQUIVALENCE PROBLEMS

Language and sequence equivalence problems of DOL systems are somewhat different but still closely related. The difference is due to the fact that two DOL systems may generate the same language in a different order, a typical example being the two systems

$$(\{a, b\}, \{a \to b^2, b \to a\}, b) \text{ and } (\{a, b\}, \{a \to b, b \to a^2\}, a).$$

That the two problems mentioned are closely related is very well illustrated by the fact that, several years before either one was known to be decidable, it was known that the decidability of one of them implies the decidability of the other.

We shall first prove the decidability of the DOL sequence equivalence problem. In fact, most of the apparatus needed for this was developed already in Chapter 4. To point out the difficulties involved, we begin with several examples.

Consider first the two DOL systems

$$G_1 = (\{a, b\}, \{a \to aba, b \to \lambda\}, aba),$$
$$G_2 = (\{a, b\}, \{a \to a, b \to ba^2b\}, aba).$$

It is easy to see that

$$L(G_1) = L(G_2) = \{(aba)^{2^n} \mid n \geq 0\}$$

and that $S(G_1) = S(G_2)$ consists of the words in $L(G_1)$ in their increasing length order. Hence, G_1 and G_2 are both language and sequence equivalent.

The ad hoc arguments like the one in the previous example cannot be extended to the general case. Regarding sequence equivalence, one can generate words from two sequences $S(G_1)$ and $S(G_2)$ one at a time, always testing whether the ith words in the two sequences coincide, for $i = 1, 2, \ldots$. This procedure constitutes a "semialgorithm" for nonequivalence: if G_1 and G_2 are *not* sequence equivalent, the procedure terminates with the correct answer. But if G_1 and G_2 are, in fact, sequence equivalent, the procedure does not terminate.

To convert this procedure into an algorithm, we would have to be able to compute a number $C(G_1, G_2)$ such that if the first $C(G_1, G_2)$ terms in $S(G_1)$ and $S(G_2)$ coincide, then $S(G_1) = S(G_2)$. However, this has turned out to be a very difficult task although, on the other hand, it might be the case that twice the size of the alphabet of G_1 and G_2 suffices. At least no examples contradicting this assumption are known. Indeed, the following example (which can be extended to bigger alphabets, cf. Exercise 1) is the "nastiest" known of two DOL systems G_1 and G_2 such that $S(G_1) \neq S(G_2)$ but as many as possible (relative to the size of the alphabet) first words in the two sequences coincide.

Consider two DOL systems G_1 and G_2 with the axiom ab. The productions for G_1 (resp. G_2) are

$$a \rightarrow abb, \; b \rightarrow aabba \; (\text{resp.} \; a \rightarrow abbaabb, \; b \rightarrow a).$$

The reader may verify that the sequences $S(G_1)$ and $S(G_2)$ coincide with respect to the first three words but are different from the fourth word on.

After these examples, we go into the general solution of the DOL sequence equivalence problem. We say that two morphisms g and h (defined on Σ^*) are *equal* on a language $L \subseteq \Sigma^*$ if $g(w) = h(w)$ holds for every w in L.

Clearly, g and h are equal on L if and only if $L \subseteq E(g, h)$, where E denotes the equality set as defined in Chapter 4.

We first prove two lemmas.

Lemma 5.1. There is an algorithm for deciding whether or not two given morphisms g and h are equal on a given regular language R.

Proof.   Let A be a finite deterministic automaton representing $R \subseteq \Sigma^*$. Consider paths in A from the initial node to one of the final nodes. Let w be a nonempty word causing a loop in such a path, i.e., w is a word such that all of the words $w_1 w^n w_2$, $n \geq 0$, are in R, for some words w_1 and w_2. Then we claim that either

$$|g(w)| - |h(w)| = 0, \tag{5.2}$$

or else g and h are not equal on R. Indeed, if (5.2) is not satisfied then, for sufficiently large values of n,

$$|g(w_1 w^n w_2)| - |h(w_1 w^n w_2)| \neq 0. \tag{5.3}$$

But since all words $w_1 w^n w_2$ are in R, (5.3) implies that g and h are not equal on R.

Consider now subsets $E_k(g, h)$ of $E(g, h)$, as defined in Exercise 4.8. Let t be the number of nodes in A and denote

$$u = max \{ ||g(a)| - |h(a)|| \},$$

where a ranges over Σ. (Here the outmost vertical bars stand for absolute value.) We restrict our attention among the sets $E_k(g, h)$ to a fixed one satisfying

$$k \geq u(t - 1)/2.$$

Clearly, we can decide whether or not

$$R \subseteq E_k(g, h). \tag{5.4}$$

(This follows because both are regular languages. Cf. Exercise 4.8 and Theorems 2.7–2.8.) If (5.4) is satisfied, then clearly g and h are equal on R. Conversely, if g and h are equal on R, then (5.2) holds for all words w causing a loop in a path from the initial node to a final node. This result implies that (5.4) is satisfied. Indeed, we know by our assumption that $R \subseteq E(g, h)$. We also know, by (5.2), that the absolute value of the difference

$$|g(x)| - |h(x)|,$$

where x is a prefix of a word in R, cannot exceed our specific number k. These observations show the correctness of (5.4). $\square$

Lemma 5.2.   It is decidable whether or not a given DOL language L is contained in a given regular language R.

Proof.   Assume that $L = L(G)$, where $G = (\Sigma, h, w)$ is a DOL system, and that R is represented by a finite deterministic automaton A. We may assume without loss of generality that Σ is also the alphabet of labels of A.

We now construct a sequence of automata $A(h)$, $A(h^2)$, $A(h^3)$, ... as follows. For each $A(h^i)$, the set of nodes, the initial and final nodes, as well as the label alphabet coincide with the corresponding items in A. (This fact implies that all automata in our sequence cannot be distinct, which information will be very useful below.) There is in $A(h^i)$ an arrow labeled by a from a node s to a node s' if and only if there is in A a path labeled by $h^i(a)$ from s to s'. Clearly, this designation specifies the automaton $A(h^i)$. Moreover, $R = h^i(R_i)$, where R_i is the language represented by $A(h^i)$.

Since all automata in our sequence are not distinct, there are numbers i and j, $i < j$, such that $A(h^i) = A(h^j)$. This fact implies that

$$A(h^{i+k}) = A(h^{j+k}),$$

for all k. Consequently, every automaton in our original sequence of automata is among the automata

$$A(h), A(h^2), \ldots, A(h^j). \tag{5.5}$$

(The automata (5.5) need not all be distinct.)

Let now R_1 be the intersection of the languages represented by the automata (5.5) and A, i.e.,

$$R_1 = \bigcap_{t=0}^{j} L(A(h^t)),$$

where $A(h^0) = A$. Clearly, we can effectively construct an automaton A_1 representing R_1. (This consequence follows by Theorem 2.7 and the fact that j can be computed effectively.)

We claim now that $L \subseteq R$ if and only if $w \in L(A_1)$. (Clearly, the latter condition is decidable.)

Indeed, $L \subseteq R$ holds if and only if $h^i(w)$ is in $L(A)$, for every $i \geq 0$. The latter condition holds if and only if w is in $L(A(h^i))$, for every $i \geq 0$, which in turn is satisfied if and only if w is in $L(A_1)$. $\square$

We are now ready to establish the first major result on the road leading to the decidability of the DOL sequence equivalence.

Theorem 5.3. It is decidable whether or not two given elementary morphisms are equal on a given DOL language.

Proof. To decide whether or not two elementary morphisms g_1 and g_2 are equal on a language $L(G)$, where $G = (\Sigma, h, w)$ is a DOL system, we proceed as follows. By Theorem 4.13, $E(g_1, g_2)$ is regular. Let $R_0, R_1, R_2, \ldots$ be an effective enumeration of all regular languages over Σ. (Such an enumeration is clearly possible. For instance, we might first consider finite deterministic automata with one node, then with two nodes, and so forth.)

We now consider two semialgorithms, one for equality, and the other for nonequality. The latter one is obvious: we consider the sequence

$$w = h^0(w), h^1(w), h^2(w), \ldots,$$

and check whether or not

$$g_1(h^i(w)) = g_2(h^i(w)).$$

If the morphisms g_1 and g_2 are not equal on $L(G)$, this semialgorithm terminates with the correct answer.

The $(i + 1)$st step in the semialgorithm for equality consists of checking, by Lemma 5.1, whether or not g_1 and g_2 are equal on R_i and, in case of a positive answer, of checking further whether or not $L(G)$ is contained in R_i. The latter checking can be accomplished by Lemma 5.2, and a positive answer implies that g_1 and g_2 are equal on $L(G)$. (In case of a negative answer to either question, we go to the $(i + 2)$nd step.) If the morphisms g_1 and g_2 are equal on $L(G)$, this semialgorithm terminates with the correct answer.

An algorithm for Theorem 5.3 is now obtained by running concurrently (i.e., taking one step from each, by turns) the two semialgorithms.   □

Instead of the abstract sequence R_i, $i = 0, 1, 2, \ldots$, in the preceding proof, we may consider the specific sequence of regular languages $E_i(g_1, g_2)$, as defined in Exercise 4.8. Then the $(i + 1)$st step in our final algorithm consists first of checking whether or not $g_1(h^i(w)) = g_2(h^i(w))$ and second, if the answer is positive, checking whether or not $L(G) \subseteq E_i(g_1, g_2)$. Of course, we would get a very simple algorithm, based on Lemma 5.2 only, if we could effectively determine the regular language $E(g_1, g_2)$. (Recall that our construction of the automaton A in the proof of Theorem 4.9 was not effective.)

The DOL sequence equivalence problem can be reduced to Theorem 5.3. The basic idea in this reduction is to decompose the morphism of an arbitrary DOL system in such a way that it suffices to test the equality of elementary morphisms on a DOL language. A useful tool in this reduction is the following lemma.

Lemma 5.4. Assume that h_1 and h_2 are morphisms of Σ^* into Σ^*. Then there is a sequence $i_1, \ldots, i_m$ of elements from $\{1, 2\}$ and morphisms f, p_1, p_2 such that

$$h_j h_{i_1} \cdots h_{i_m} = p_j f, \qquad j = 1, 2, \tag{5.6}$$

and the morphisms p_j are elementary. Moreover, the sequence $i_1, \ldots, i_m$ and the morphisms f, p_1, p_2 can be effectively constructed.

Proof. If both h_1 and h_2 are elementary, we choose $p_j = h_j$, $j = 1, 2$. We choose f to be the identity morphism, and the sequence of elements from $\{1, 2\}$ the empty one.

Assume at least one of h_1 and h_2 is not elementary. Consider a product, formed of h_1 and h_2, giving rise to a simplification

$$h_{i_1} \cdots h_{i_m} = gf \tag{5.7}$$

via a smallest possible alphabet for all such products. More specifically, we assume that (5.7) holds with

$$f : \Sigma^* \to \Sigma_1^* \quad \text{and} \quad g : \Sigma_1^* \to \Sigma^*,$$

where the subalphabet Σ_1 is of smaller cardinality than Σ, and whenever

$$h_{j_1} \cdots h_{j_n} = g_1 f_1, \; f_1 : \Sigma^* \to \Sigma_2^*, \; g_1 : \Sigma_2^* \to \Sigma^*,$$

then Σ_2 is not of smaller cardinality than Σ_1.

Define now $p_j = h_j g$, $j = 1, 2$. Then (5.7) yields (5.6). Moreover, the minimality of Σ_1 guarantees that p_1 and p_2 are elementary. Indeed, if $h_j g$ possesses a simplification

$$h_j g = g' g'',$$

then we obtain

$$h_j h_{i_1} \cdots h_{i_m} = g'(g'' f),$$

which is a product of the h's giving rise to a simplification via an alphabet of a cardinality smaller than that of Σ_1.

The construction is effective because, given any sequence $i_1, \ldots, i_m$, we can check whether (5.6) holds for some elementary p_j. (It is easy to decide whether or not a given morphism is elementary, cf. Exercise 2.) Thus, we just go systematically through all sequences until we find a correct one. The first part of the proof guarantees that we will eventually succeed. □

We now have all the apparatus available to establish the main result.

Theorem 5.5. The DOL sequence equivalence problem is decidable.

Proof. We assume without loss of generality that the given DOL systems are

$$G_i = (\Sigma, h_i, w), i = 1, 2,$$

i.e., the initial words and the alphabets coincide. Denote the words in the sequences $S(G_i)$, $i = 1, 2$, as follows:

$$w = w_0^{(i)}, w_1^{(i)}, w_2^{(i)}, \ldots .$$

Let now $i_1, \ldots, i_m, p_1, p_2, f$ satisfy Lemma 5.4 for h_1 and h_2. Denote

$$g_i = h_i h_{i_1} \cdots h_{i_m} = p_i f, i = 1, 2,$$

and consider the DOL systems

$$G_{ij} = (\Sigma, g_i, w_j^{(i)}), 1 \leq i \leq 2, 0 \leq j \leq m.$$

(Observe that Σ may contain letters not actually occurring in $S(G_{ij})$. However, the morphisms g_i are defined on the whole Σ.)

Clearly, if $S(G_1) = S(G_2)$, then also

$$S(G_{1j}) = S(G_{2j}) \text{ for all } j, \text{ where } 0 \leq j \leq m. \tag{5.8}$$

But also the converse implication holds, as seen indirectly by the following argument. Assume that (5.8) holds but that there is an integer n with the property $w_n^{(1)} \neq w_n^{(2)}$. We choose n to be the smallest integer with this property. Clearly we cannot have $n \leq m$ because then the first elements of the sequences $S(G_{1n})$ and $S(G_{2n})$ would be different, a contradiction. Thus, $n \geq m + 1$. Choosing now an integer t such that

$$0 \leq n_1 = n - t(m + 1) \leq m,$$

we see that the $(t + 1)$st words in the sequences $S(G_{1n_1})$ and $S(G_{2n_1})$ are different, which is also a contradiction.

Thus, to complete the proof, we need only to show the decidability of the equations (5.8). For this purpose, we consider a fixed j and denote

$$H_i = G_{ij} = (\Sigma, g_i, w_j^{(i)}), i = 1, 2.$$

We consider also the morphisms p_1, p_2, f introduced earlier in this proof. We may assume that $w_j^{(1)} = w_j^{(2)}$ and, consequently, $f(w_j^{(1)}) = f(w_j^{(2)})$ because, otherwise, $S(H_1) \neq S(H_2)$ and we are through.

Consider now the DOL systems

$$K_i = (\Sigma_i, fp_i, f(w_j^{(i)})), i = 1, 2,$$

where Σ_i is the subalphabet of Σ through which g_i is simplified. (Here we have to take a subalphabet because fp_i is not necessarily defined on the whole Σ.)

By Theorem 2.3, we can decide whether or not p_1 and p_2 are equal on $L(K_1)$. But it is an immediate consequence of the definitions that p_1 and p_2 are equal on $L(K_1)$ if and only if $S(H_1) = S(H_2)$. $\square$

The proof of the decidability of the language equivalence problem for DOL systems does not contain any essentially new language-theoretic ideas and is, therefore, omitted. Essentially, in this proof one associates with a given DOL system $G = (\Sigma, h, w)$ systems of the form

$$G(p, q) = (\Sigma_{pq}, h^p, h^q(w)),$$

where the "period" p is large enough to ensure a unique order among the words, so that Theorem 5.5 becomes applicable. When running the algorithm, one tries to reduce the period at the cost of making the "initial mess" q larger. Regarding references to the details of the proof of the following theorem, the reader is referred to Exercise 5.

Theorem 5.6. The language equivalence problem for DOL systems is decidable.

5.3   UNDECIDABILITY RESULTS

We now apply reduction to the Post correspondence problem to show that Theorem 5.6 cannot be extended to concern OL systems. At the same time we get the result that the language equivalence problem for context-free grammars (cf. Chapter 2) is undecidable. Both results are consequences of the following lemma.

By a *sentential form* of a grammar we mean any word α such that $S \Rightarrow *\alpha$, for some start letter S. Thus, sentential forms may consist of both terminals and nonterminals, whereas the language $L(G)$ generated by a grammar G consists of words over the terminal alphabet only.

Lemma 5.7.   It is undecidable whether or not two given context-free grammars generate the same set of sentential forms.

Proof.   We argue indirectly, assuming that there is an algorithm for deciding whether or not two given context-free grammars generate the same sentential forms. This algorithm is applied in the following way to solve the Post correspondence problem, which shows that our assumption must be wrong.

Consider an arbitrary instance

$$g : \Sigma^* \to \Sigma_1^*, h : \Sigma^* \to \Sigma_1^*$$

of the Post correspondence problem, where we denote

$$\Sigma = \{a_1, \ldots, a_m\}, \Sigma_1 = \{b_1, \ldots, b_n\}.$$

We introduce three languages L, L_g and L_h over the alphabet

$$\Sigma \cup \Sigma_1 \cup \{\#\}.$$

By definition,

$$L = \Sigma^* \# \Sigma_1^*.$$

The language L_g is the subset of L, consisting of all words in L, with the exception of words of the form

$$w \# g\,(mi(w)), w \neq \lambda, \tag{5.9}$$

where $mi(x)$ denotes the *mirror image* of the word x, i.e., x written backwards. (If x is λ or consists of a single letter only, then $mi(x) = x$.) The language L_h is defined in the same way, with h instead of g in (5.9).

Clearly,

$$L = L_g \cup L_h \text{ if and only if } E(g, h) = \phi. \tag{5.10}$$

(Recall that $E(g, h)$ is considered to be empty if it consists of the empty word alone.) Using our initial assumption, we now give an algorithm for deciding whether or not $L = L_g \cup L_h$. By (5.10), this algorithm works also for the Post correspondence problem.

We define two context-free grammars G_1 and G_2 as follows. The only start letter for both grammars is S_0 and the nonterminal (resp. terminal) alphabet is

$$\{S_0, S_1, S_2, S_3, S_4, A, B\} \quad (\text{resp. } \Sigma \cup \Sigma_1 \cup \{\#\}).$$

The productions of G_1 are listed below. In the list it is understood that a runs through Σ and b through Σ_1.

$$S_0 \to A, \; S_0 \to B, \; S_0 \to S_4, S_0 \to \#,$$
$$A \to aAg(a), \; B \to aBh(a),$$
$$A \to S_3b, \; B \to S_3b,$$
$$A \to aS_1x, \; B \to aS_1y,$$

where x (resp. y) runs through all words over Σ_1 shorter than $g(a)$ (resp. $h(a)$), including the empty word,

$$A \to aS_2x, \; B \to aS_2y,$$

where x (resp. y) runs through all words over Σ_1 of the length $|g(a)|$ (resp. $|h(a)|$) but different from $g(a)$ (resp. $h(a)$),

$$S_1 \to aS_1, \; S_1 \to \#,$$
$$S_2 \to aS_2, \; S_2 \to S_3,$$
$$S_3 \to S_3b, \; S_3 \to \#,$$
$$S_4 \to aS_4, \; S_4 \to S_4b.$$

The productions of G_2 are obtained from those of G_1 by replacing the two productions $S_1 \to \#$ and $S_3 \to \#$ with the production $S_4 \to \#$. This concludes the definition of G_1 and G_2.

It is now immediately verified that G_1 and G_2 generate the same sentential forms, with the possible exception of words strictly over the terminal alphabet. Hence, because we can decide whether or not the sets of sentential forms generated by G_1 and G_2 coincide, we can also decide whether or not $L(G_1) = L(G_2)$.

Clearly, $L(G_2) = L$. In fact, L is derived according to G_2 using only the nonterminals S_0 and S_4. By (5.10) and because we can decide whether or not $L(G_1) = L(G_2)$, it suffices to show that

$$L(G_1) = L_g \cup L_h \qquad (5.11)$$

to complete the proof of Lemma 5.7.

We establish (5.11) by showing the inclusion in both directions. Assume that w is a word in $L(G_1)$. We want to show that w is in $L_g \cup L_h$. This holds true if $w = \#$. Thus, assume $w \neq \#$. Because S_4 cannot be eliminated, we conclude that the first production applied in the derivation of w is $S_0 \to A$ or $S_0 \to B$. Since the situation is symmetric, it suffices to consider the first alternative and to show that w is in L_g. The sequence of distinct nonterminals appearing in the derivation of w from A must be one of the following sequences:

$$(A, S_3), (A, S_1), (A, S_2, S_3). \qquad (5.12)$$

In each of these cases, it is immediately verified that w is in L_g. (In the first case, the part of the word coming after the center marker $\#$ is "too long." In the second case, it is "too short." In the third case, an error has been found in the matching between a and $g(a)$.)

Assume, conversely, that w is in $L_g \cup L_h$, say, in L_g. If $w \in \# \Sigma_1^*$, we can generate w according to G_1, using the productions

$$S_0 \to \#, \; S_0 \to A, \; A \to S_3 b, \; S_3 \to S_3 b, \; S_3 \to \#.$$

Thus, we may assume that

$$w = a_{i_1} \cdots a_{i_k} \# w', \; k \geq 1, \; w' \in \Sigma_1^*, \; w' \neq g(a_{i_k} \cdots a_{i_1}).$$

Let u be the greatest integer in the interval $0 \leq u \leq k$ such that $w' = w_1 g(a_{i_u} \cdots a_{i_1})$.

Assume first that $u = 0$, i.e., w' is not of the form $w' = w_1 g(a_{i_1})$. If $|w'| < |g(a_{i_1})|$, we can generate w using the productions

$$S_0 \to A, \; A \to a_{i_1} S_1 w', \; S_1 \to a S_1, \; S_1 \to \#.$$

If $|w'| \geq |g(a_{i_1})|$, we write $w' = w''x$ where $|x| = |g(a_{i_1})|$ and $x \neq g(a_{i_1})$. We can now generate w using the productions

$$S_0 \rightarrow A, \ A \rightarrow a_{i_1} S_2 x, \ S_2 \rightarrow a\, S_2, \ S_2 \rightarrow S_3,$$
$$S_3 \rightarrow S_3 b, \ S_3 \rightarrow \#.$$

Assume, secondly, that $u = k$. In this case w' is of the form

$$w' = w_1 g(a_{i_k} \cdots a_{i_1}).$$

Furthermore, we must have $w_1 \neq \lambda$ because, otherwise, w would not be in L_g. The word w can now be generated with the productions

$$S_0 \rightarrow A, \ A \rightarrow aAg(a), \ A \rightarrow S_3 b, \ S_3 \rightarrow S_3 b, \ S_3 \rightarrow \#.$$

Assume, finally, that $1 \leq u < k$. Consequently, there is a word w_1 such that

$$w' = w_1 g(a_{i_u} \cdots a_{i_1})$$

but no word w_2 such that

$$w' = w_2 g(a_{i_{u+1}} \cdots a_{i_1}). \tag{5.13}$$

If $|w_1| < |g(a_{i_{u+1}})|$, we can generate w using the productions

$$S_0 \rightarrow A, \ A \rightarrow aAg(a), \ A \rightarrow a_{i_{u+1}} S_1 w_1, \ S_1 \rightarrow aS_1, \ S_1 \rightarrow \#.$$

Otherwise, we can write w_1 in the form $w_1 = w_3 x$, where $|x| = |g(a_{i_{u+1}})|$ and $x \neq g(a_{i_{u+1}})$. (Recall that w' is not of the form (5.13).) The word w can now be generated with the productions

$$S_0 \rightarrow A, \ A \rightarrow aAg(a), \ A \rightarrow a_{i_{u+1}} S_2 x, \ S_2 \rightarrow aS_2, \ S_2 \rightarrow S_3, \ S_3 \rightarrow S_3 b, \ S_3 \rightarrow \#.$$

Hence, we have shown in all cases that w is in $L(G_1)$. $\square$

The above proof shows that we cannot decide whether or not G_1 and G_2 generate the same sentential forms. We can transform G_1 and G_2 into OL systems by adding the production $c \rightarrow c$, for every terminal letter c. Hence, the language equivalence problem is undecidable for OL systems. (In fact, it remains undecidable even if attention is restricted to a special class of OL systems, namely, those of the form of G_1 and G_2. For instance, no λ-productions are needed.)

But the above proof shows also that we cannot decide whether or not $L(G_1) = L(G_2)$, when G_1 and G_2 are viewed as context-free grammars. Hence, the language equivalence problem for context-free grammars is undecidable. Our argument shows, in fact, that it remains undecidable if attention is restricted to *linear* grammars, where no production contains more than one nonterminal on the right side.

Thus, the following result is a corollary of Lemma 5.7.

Theorem 5.8.   The language equivalence problem for OL systems is undecidable. The language equivalence problem for context-free grammars is undecidable.

EXERCISES

1. An example was given in the text of DOL systems G_1 and G_2 with an alphabet of cardinality 2 such that the first three words in the sequences $S(G_1)$ and $S(G_2)$ coincide but the fourth words do not coincide any more. Generalize this example to systems with alphabets of cardinality $2n$. In this case, the first $3n$ words in the sequences must coincide.

2. Give an algorithm for deciding whether or not a morphism $g : \Sigma^* \to \Sigma_1^*$ is elementary. (A straightforward algorithm consists of a systematic check through alphabets of cardinality smaller than that of Σ, each time trying out all possible decompositions. Try to construct a more efficient algorithm than this straightforward one.)

3. Compute an upper bound for the number m in Lemma 5.4.

4. Prove the existence of a number $C(G_1, G_2)$, computable from the DOL systems G_1 and G_2, such that G_1 and G_2 are sequence equivalent if and only if $S(G_1)$ and $S(G_2)$ coincide with respect to the first $C(G_1, G_2)$ words. (You may want to consult [EhR 3] for details. Note that our proof of Theorem 5.5, which uses two semialgorithms running concurrently, does not directly yield any such number $C(G_1, G_2)$.)

5. Using Theorem 5.5, give a detailed proof of Theorem 5.6. (The reduction of language equivalence to sequence equivalence, as well as the converse reduction, was first given in [Nie]. A simpler argument appears in [RS].)

6. Assume that an algorithm is known for deciding whether two given DOL systems satisfying the additional condition for generating ω-words generate, in fact, the same ω-word. (Cf. Exercise 1.15.) Show how such an algorithm can be used to solve the DOL sequence equivalence problem also.

7. In general, the decidability of the language inclusion problem implies the decidability of the language equivalence problem, but not vice versa. Show that even the language inclusion problem is decidable for DOL systems. (Cf. [Ru 2].)

8. The argument in the proof of Lemma 5.7 can be used to establish several other undecidability results. Prove along these lines the undecidability of the following problems. (i) Is a given OL language regular? (ii) Is a given context-free language regular? (iii) Is a given context-free language equal to a given regular language? (iv) Is the complement of a given context-free language empty? (v) Is the intersection of two given context-free languages empty? (vi) Is the intersection of two given context-free languages finite? (vii) Is the intersection of two given context-free languages regular? (viii) Problems (v)–(vii) stated for two given OL languages.

9. Show that each of the following problems is decidable. (i) Is a given context-free language equal to a given DOL language? (ii) Is a given DOL language context-free? (iii) Is a given context-free language DOL? (For (i)–(iii), cf. [Sa 4] and [Li 2].) (iv) Is a given OL language equal to a given DOL language? (Cf. [Ru 1].)

   Problem (iv) above gives a considerable extension of Theorem 5.6. Decision problems comparative between two language classes, such as (i) and (iv) above and (iii) in Exercise 8, are often investigated to sharpen the borderline between decidable and undecidable. Problems (ii) and (iii) above and (i) and (ii) in Exercise 8 are examples of comparative decision problems of a different kind: two language classes are considered, and one has to decide whether or not a given language from one class belongs to the other class.

10. Show that the finiteness problem is decidable for OL languages. (Emptiness and finiteness problems are decidable for context-free languages as well. Cf. [Sa 2], where also a survey concerning decidability and undecidability in the Chomsky hierarchy is given.)

11. Prove that it is decidable whether or not two given (arbitrary) morphisms g and h are equal on a given context-free language L. (Cf. [CuS].) Prove that the equation $g(L) = h(L)$ is undecidable in this set-up.

12. The decidability status of the following generalization of the DOL sequence equivalence problem is still open. We are given two n-tuples of morphisms

$$(g_1, \ldots, g_n), (h_1, \ldots, h_n),$$

where each morphism maps Σ^* into Σ^*, and also a word w in Σ^*. We have to decide whether or not

$$g_{i_1} \cdots g_{i_k}(w) = h_{i_1} \cdots h_{i_k}(w)$$

holds for all sequences $i_1, \ldots, i_k$ of numbers from $\{1, \ldots, n\}$. Prove that this problem is decidable if and only if it is decidable in the special case that $n = 2$.

13. Investigate the decidability status of the following problem. (At the time of this writing the problem is still open.) Consider an OL system $G = (\Sigma, \sigma, w)$. Each finite sequence of words

$$w_0, w_1, \ldots, w_n, \; n \geq 0,$$

where $w_0 = w$ and w_{i+1} is in $\sigma(w_i)$, for $0 \leq i \leq n - 1$, is referred to as a *developmental history* according to G. Denote by $DH(G)$ the set of all developmental histories according to G. Construct an algorithm for deciding whether or not

$$DH(G_1) = DH(G_2)$$

holds for two given OL systems G_1 and G_2.

Chapter 6

MORPHIC REPRESENTATIONS

6.1 LOCAL AND REGULAR LANGUAGES

The notion of a basis or a set of generators occurs quite frequently in mathematical considerations. The idea is that a class of objects is characterized by choosing some "basic" or "atomic" ones in this class and then showing that every object is obtainable from the basic ones by applying certain operations and, on the other hand, these operations do not lead outside the original class. In other words, the original class equals the closure of the basis with respect to the operations.

Language theory abounds with such characterization results. In this chapter we shall focus attention to characterizations where the operations considered are morphisms or inverse morphisms. Particularly interesting will be the case where an important class of languages, such as a class in the Chomsky hierarchy, is generated from a single language by just one application of a morphic operation.

We shall first present some simple results concerning the family of regular languages. We begin with several definitions.

Consider a morphism $h : \Sigma^* \rightarrow \Sigma_1^*$. The mapping g of Σ_1^* into the set of subsets of Σ^* such that

$$g(w) = \{w' \,|\, h(w') = w\} \tag{6.1}$$

is termed the *inverse* of h and denoted $g = h^{-1}$. Mappings of the form (6.1) are referred to as *inverse morphisms*. For a language L over Σ_1, we define

$$g(L) = h^{-1}(L) = \{w \,|\, h(w) \in L\}.$$

Let Σ be an alphabet, let A and B be subsets of Σ, and let C be a subset of Σ^2. Then, by Theorem 2.7, the language

96

$$L = A\Sigma^* \cap \Sigma^* B \setminus \Sigma^* C \Sigma^* \qquad (6.2)$$

is regular. Languages L of the form (6.2), for some Σ, A, B, C, are referred to as *local*.

The term "local" originates from the fact that if L is a language of the form (6.2), then it suffices to scan an arbitrary word w locally to find out whether or not w is in L. Indeed, assume that w is written on a tape divided into squares, each letter occupying one square. Assume, further, that you have a ruler with a hole the size of two tape squares. Then, by moving the ruler to different positions, you are able to tell whether or not w is in L, without remembering anything other than A, B, C and Σ. For clearly the size of the hole allows you to tell where w begins and ends, and so you can check to see that correct letters are in these positions. You can also check that no forbidden subwords of length 2 (i.e., words in C) appear.

Local languages are also referred to as "2-testable," reflecting the length of the local scans, i.e., the size of the hole. An analogous definition can be given for k-testable languages. Essentially, we are then considering a hole from which k adjacent squares can be seen.

Local languages are closely related with finite deterministic automata, as seen from the proof of the following simple result.

Theorem 6.1. Every regular language R not containing the empty word λ can be expressed in the form

$$R = h(L), \qquad (6.3)$$

where L is local and h is a letter-to-letter morphism. Every regular language R_0 containing λ can be expressed in the form

$$R_0 = h(L \cup \{\lambda\}),$$

where h and L are as before.

Proof. Clearly, the second sentence is a consequence of the first sentence. (Observe that a local language never contains λ.) To prove the first sentence, we consider a finite deterministic automaton G representing $R \subseteq \Sigma_1^*$. Let Σ be the alphabet, where the letters are labeled edges of G. That is, the elements of Σ are triples (s, a, s') such that there is in G an edge labeled by the letter a from the node s to the node s'.

Consider now the language (6.2), where A (resp. B) consists of those triples (s, a, s') such that s is the initial node (resp. s' is a final node), and

$$C = \{(s, a, s\,')(s_1, a_1, s_1\,') \,|\, s\,' \neq s_1 \}.$$

Let $h : \Sigma^* \to \Sigma_1^*$ be the letter-to-letter morphism defined by the condition

$$h((s, a, s\,')) = a.$$

It is now an immediate consequence of our definitions that (6.3) is satisfied.   □

The simplicity of the previous argument is due to the appropriate characterization of regular languages. The reader might think about a proof not applying finite automata and assuming that R is given by a regular expression!

The main results in this chapter will be that every context-free (resp. recursively enumerable) language L can be represented in the form $L = h_L^{-1}(L_0)$, where L_0 is a fixed context-free (resp. recursively enumerable) language and h_L is a morphism, depending on L. (If L contains the empty word, we need a slight modification of this statement.) A similar result holds for context-sensitive languages as well. We now show that no analogous result holds for the fourth family in the Chomsky hierarchy, namely, the family of regular languages. In fact, we obtain a slightly stronger result. A morphic characterization using equality sets is given for regular languages in Exercise 12.

Theorem 6.2. There is no regular language R_0 such that every regular language R (not containing the empty word) can be represented in the form $R = h_1(h_2^{-1}(R_0))$, where h_1 and h_2 are morphisms.

Proof. We argue indirectly and assume that such an R_0 exists. Let R_0 be represented by a finite deterministic automaton with n nodes. Then every language of the form $h_2^{-1}(R_0)$ is represented by a finite deterministic automaton with n nodes. (The reader is reminded of the construction of the automaton $A(h)$ in the proof of Lemma 5.2.) But a language represented by a finite deterministic automaton with n nodes is of star height $\leq n$. (This is seen, for instance, by considering the languages $L(i, j, k)$ in the proof of Theorem 2.9.) Consequently, all languages of the form $h_2^{-1}(R_0)$ are of star height $\leq n$. Clearly, a morphic image of a language of star height m is itself of star height $\leq m$. (Observe that if a language is denoted by a regular expression α, then its morphic image is denoted by a regular expression obtained from α by replacing every letter with its morphic image.) This implies, finally, that every language of the form $h_1(h_2^{-1}(R_0))$ is of star height $\leq n$, which contradicts Theorem 3.2.   □

6.2 A MORPHIC GENERATOR FOR CONTEXT-FREE LANGUAGES

In this section, we shall explicitly construct a context-free language L_0 such that every context-free language L is representable in the form $h^{-1}(L_0)$, for some morphism h. Intuitively, all possible derivations of all context-free grammars appear in an encoded form in L_0; the morphism is used to pick up the end results of the correct derivations.

We present first some "normal form" results for context-free grammars: it is shown that every context-free language can be generated by a grammar whose productions are of a specific form. The normal forms given in Lemmas 6.3 and 6.4 are usually referred to as the *Chomsky* and *Greibach normal forms*, respectively. Only brief descriptive proofs are given for these lemmas. The reader might like to fill in the missing details. Besides, more detailed arguments appear in a number of books, for instance, in [Sa2]. We use the short expression "λ-free language" to mean a language not containing λ. In considering grammars, we use capital (resp. small) letters from the beginning of the alphabet, possibly provided with indices or primes, to denote nonterminals (resp. terminals).

Lemma 6.3.   Every λ-free context-free language is generated by a grammar with productions of the two forms $A \to BC$ and $A \to a$ only.

Proof.   We perform a sequence of transformations to the given grammar, each of which leaves the language of the grammar invariant, such that the end result is of the required form. Clearly, we may assume that the given grammar has just one start letter S.

We begin with eliminating the productions $A \to \lambda$. For this aim, we first determine the set U consisting of all nonterminals B such that $B \Rightarrow *\lambda$. The new set of productions consists now of all productions $A \to \alpha_1$, $\alpha_1 \neq \lambda$, such that there is a production $A \to \alpha$ in the old set of productions and α_1 is obtained from α by deleting 0 or more occurrences of elements of U.

In essentially the same way, we can now get rid of the productions $A \to B$. We first determine, for each nonterminal A, the set U_A consisting of all terminals and nonterminals x such that $A \Rightarrow *x$. (Recall that productions $A \to \lambda$ have already been eliminated. Hence, a derivation $A \Rightarrow *x$ uses length-preserving productions only.) The new set of productions consists now of, first, all productions $S \to a$, where a is a terminal in the set U_S, and, second, all productions $B \rightarrow y_1 \cdots y_n$, where $n \geq 2$ and each y is a letter, such that there is in the original set a production $A \rightarrow x_1 \cdots x_n$ with the properties

$$A \in U_B, \; y_i \in \{x_i\} \cup U_{x_i}, \; i = 1, \ldots, n.$$

(Clearly, A is always in U_A. The term $\{x_i\}$ has to be added to take care of terminals x_i.)

We now replace every terminal letter a in the productions by a new nonterminal A_a, and add the productions $A_a \rightarrow a$ to the production set. After this transformation, terminals appear in productions of the form $A \rightarrow a$ only.

After these transformations, our grammar contains only productions of the two forms $A \rightarrow a$ and

$$A \rightarrow B_1 B_2 \cdots B_n, \; n \geq 2. \tag{6.4}$$

For each production (6.4) where $n > 2$, we introduce new nonterminals $C_1, \ldots, C_{n-2}$ and replace (6.4) by the productions

$$A \rightarrow B_1 C_1, \; C_1 \rightarrow B_2 C_2, \; \ldots, \; C_{n-3} \rightarrow B_{n-2} C_{n-2}, \; C_{n-2} \rightarrow B_{n-1} B_n. \qquad \square$$

Lemma 6.4. Every λ-free context-free language L is generated by a grammar with productions of the three forms $A \rightarrow aBC$, $A \rightarrow aB$, $A \rightarrow a$ only.

Proof. We begin with a grammar for L of the form of Lemma 6.3. It will be convenient to use matrix notation in the representation of the set of productions. Assume that the nonterminals in our grammar are $A_1, \ldots, A_n$, where A_1 is the only start symbol. If

$$A_i \rightarrow \alpha_j, j = 1, \ldots, m,$$

are all the productions for A_i, we express this in the form

$$A_i \rightarrow \alpha_1 + \cdots + \alpha_m.$$

Denoting $V = (A_1, \ldots, A_n)$, we may now express the entire set of productions in the matrix form

$$V \rightarrow T + VM, \tag{6.5}$$

where (i) T is an n-dimensional row vector whose entries are sums of terminal letters and (ii) M is an n-dimensional square matrix whose entries are sums of nonterminal letters. In (i) and (ii), "empty sums" ϕ may occur.

For instance, if the productions in our grammar are

$$A_1 \rightarrow A_1 A_2 + A_1 A_1 + a + b, \, A_2 \rightarrow A_2 A_1 + A_1 A_1 + b,$$

we have in our matrix representation

$$T = (a + b, \, b), \; M = \begin{pmatrix} A_1 + A_2 & A_1 \\ \phi & A_1 \end{pmatrix}.$$

Conversely, given a matrix representation for V (not necessarily of the form (6.5)), we can write on the basis of this representation the productions in the customary form.

We now modify (6.5) in such a way that the resulting matrix representation gives rise to productions only in the form required in Lemma 6.4. For this purpose, we introduce n^2 new nonterminals B_{ij}, $1 \leq i, j \leq n$, and let Y be the square matrix $Y = (B_{ij})$. Consider the grammar

$$V \rightarrow T + TY, \, Y \rightarrow M + MY. \tag{6.6}$$

Here A_1 is still the start symbol. The productions in the second set are determined in the natural way: the right sides of the productions for B_{ij} appear in the (i, j)th entry of the matrix $M + MY$.

It is not difficult to see that also the grammar (6.6) generates our given language L. Basically, this is due to the fact that when in (6.5) productions resulting from VM are used, then the nonterminals in V must eventually terminate. This is the idea behind TY in (6.6). On the other hand, Y is capable of deriving every power of M, and so the termination can be postponed as long as needed.

More formally, assume that w is a word of length t in L. By iterating, we may write (6.5) in the forms

$$V \rightarrow T + TM + VM^2, \ldots, V \rightarrow T + TM + \cdots + TM^{t-1} + VM^t.$$

Since w is generated by (6.5) and $|w| = t$, we conclude that w is generated by the grammar

$$V \rightarrow T + TM + \cdots + TM^{t-1}. \tag{6.7}$$

(The productions obtainable from $V \rightarrow VM^t$ can be used in the derivation of words of length $>t$ only.) By similarly iterating Y in (6.6)

$$Y \rightarrow M + M^2 + \cdots + M^{t-1} + M^t Y, \tag{6.8}$$

we see that every word generated by (6.7), in particular the word w, is generated by (6.6).

Conversely, we can use (6.8) to show that if w is a word of length t generated by (6.6), then w is in L.

For $i = 1, \ldots, n$, let $Y^{(i)}$ (resp. $M^{(i)}$) be the ith row of Y (resp. M). We write (6.6) first in the form

$$V \to T + TY, \; Y^{(i)} \to M^{(i)} + M^{(i)}Y, \, i = 1, \ldots, n. \qquad (6.9)$$

Since the entries of M are sums of nonterminals, we may write

$$M^{(i)} = VT^{(i)}, \, i = 1, \ldots, n,$$

where $T^{(i)}$ is an n-dimensional square matrix all of whose entries are either λ or ϕ. This brings (6.9) to the form

$$V \to T + TY, \; Y^{(i)} \to VT^{(i)} + VT^{(i)}Y, \, i = 1, \ldots, n. \qquad (6.10)$$

Finally, when we apply $V \to T + TY$ to the other occurrences of V in (6.10), we obtain the grammar

$$V \to T + TY, \; Y^{(i)} \to TT^{(i)} + TYT^{(i)} + TT^{(i)}Y + TYT^{(i)}Y, \, i = 1, \ldots, n,$$

which clearly yields productions of the required forms only.   □

We shall now define the most important tools for recording derivations according to a context-free grammar.

Consider the alphabet

$$\Sigma = \Sigma_1 \cup \overline{\Sigma}_1, \, \overline{\Sigma}_1 = \{\overline{a} | a \in \Sigma_1 \}, \, \Sigma_1 \cap \overline{\Sigma}_1 = \phi.$$

The *Dyck mapping* ρ of Σ^* into itself is defined by

$$\rho(\lambda) = \lambda,$$

$$\rho(wa) = \rho(w)a, \text{ for all } w \in \Sigma^*, a \in \Sigma_1,$$

$$\rho(w\overline{a}) = \begin{cases} \rho(w)\overline{a} & \text{if } \rho(w) \notin \Sigma^*a, \\ w_1 & \text{if } \rho(w) = w_1a. \end{cases}$$

Assume that Σ_1 consists of $k \geq 1$ letters $a_1, \ldots, a_k$. The *Dyck language* D_k is defined by

$$D_k = \{w \mid \rho(w) = \lambda\}.$$

Thus, D_k consists of all words over Σ that can be reduced to λ by applying the equations

$$a_i \bar{a}_i = \lambda, \; i = 1, \ldots, k.$$

If we view a_i (resp. $\bar{a}_i$) as a left (resp. right) parenthesis of a certain type, then D_k consists of all sequences of "properly nested" parentheses. For instance, denoting

$$a_1 = (\; , a_2 = [\; , \bar{a}_1 = \;), \bar{a}_2 = \;],$$

we see that $[(\;)[\;]](\;)$ is in D_2, whereas $([)]$ and $(\;)[\;]]$ are not in D_2.

Clearly, D_k is generated by the context-free grammar defined by the productions

$$S \to SS, \; S \to \lambda, \; S \to a_i S \bar{a}_i, \; i = 1, \ldots, k. \tag{6.11}$$

In what follows, we shall be concerned with the Dyck language D_2 because arbitrary letters can be conveniently encoded with two letters. In fact, the following "initialized version" of D_2 will be very useful:

$$D = \bar{a}_1 \bar{a}_2 \bar{a}_1 D_2. \tag{6.12}$$

A slight modification of the grammar (6.11) generates the language D: we just add a new nonterminal S_1 (which is going to be the only start symbol) and the production $S_1 \to \bar{a}_1 \bar{a}_2 \bar{a}_1 S$. We assume that $k = 2$ in (6.11).

For a finite substitution σ, its *inverse* σ^{-1}, operating on a language L, is defined by

$$\sigma^{-1}(L) = \{w \mid \sigma(w) \cap L \neq \phi\}.$$

Observe that $\sigma(w)$ consists, in general, of several words. It is not required that they are all in the language L in order for w to be in $\sigma^{-1}(L)$; just one of them being in L is sufficient. We also point out that the domain and target alphabets were equal for the finite substitutions considered in Chapter 5. Here they may be different.

We are now ready for the first major representation result. In the statement of the theorem, D means the language (6.12). That attention is restricted to λ-free languages is unessential: languages containing λ are similarly generated from $D \cup \{\lambda\}$.

Theorem 6.5. For every λ-free context-free language L, there is a finite substitution σ such that

$$L = \sigma^{-1}(D). \qquad (6.13)$$

Proof. Consider an arbitrary L, generated by a grammar G whose production set P is in the form of Lemma 6.4. Assume that

$$\{A_1, \ldots, A_n\} \text{ and } \Sigma_L$$

are the nonterminal and terminal alphabets of G and that A_1 is the only start symbol. Recall that D is a language over the alphabet

$$\Sigma = \{a_1, a_2, \bar{a}_1, \bar{a}_2\}.$$

Intuitively, A_i will be encoded as $a_1 a_2^i a_1$, $i = 1, \ldots, n$. The word $\bar{a}_1 \bar{a}_2^i \bar{a}_1$ will be used to encode the "inverse" of A_i, meaning that an occurrence of A_i is deleted.

Formally, we define a finite substitution $\sigma : \Sigma_L{}^* \rightarrow \Sigma^*$ by

$$\sigma(b) = \{\bar{a}_1 \bar{a}_2^i \bar{a}_1 \,|\, A_i \rightarrow b \text{ is in } P\} \qquad (6.14)$$

$$\cup \{\bar{a}_1 \bar{a}_2^i \bar{a}_1 a_1 a_2^j a_1 \,|\, A_i \rightarrow bA_j \text{ is in } P\}$$

$$\cup \{\bar{a}_1 \bar{a}_2^i \bar{a}_1 a_1 a_2^k a_1 a_1 a_2^j a_1 \,|\, A_i \rightarrow bA_jA_k \text{ is in } P\},$$

where b is an arbitrary letter of Σ_L, and i, j, k range over $\{1, \ldots, n\}$. We still have to show that (6.13) holds. For this purpose, it is convenient to establish a somewhat stronger assertion.

For $i = 1, \ldots, n$, let L_i be the language generated by the productions P from the start symbol A_i. We, thus, consider grammars obtained from G by changing the start symbol, and observe that $L_1 = L$. We shall establish the following:

Assertion. Assume that $1 \leq i \leq n$ and w is an arbitrary word over Σ_L. Then w is in L_i if and only if $\sigma(w)$ contains a word in

$$\bar{a}_1 \bar{a}_2^i \bar{a}_1 D_2, \qquad (6.15)$$

i.e., if and only if w is in $\sigma^{-1}(\bar{a}_1 \bar{a}_2^i \bar{a}_1 D_2)$.

Observe first that (6.13) follows from our assertion, by choosing $i = 1$. The proof of the assertion is by induction on the length t of the word w. We may assume $t \geq 1$: the empty word does not belong to any of the languages considered. (Cf. also Exercise 5.)

As the basis of induction, consider the case $t = 1$. Then w is in L_i if and only if $A_i \rightarrow w$ is in P, which happens if and only if

$$\bar{a}_1 \bar{a}_2^i \bar{a}_1 \in \sigma(w). \tag{6.16}$$

Since $\bar{a}_1 \bar{a}_2^i \bar{a}_1$ is the only word on the right side of (6.14) belonging also to the language (6.15), we conclude that (6.16) holds if and only if $\sigma(w)$ contains a word in (6.15). Hence, w is in L_i if and only if $\sigma(w)$ contains a word in (6.15).

As an inductive hypothesis, assume that our assertion holds for all words of length smaller than t (≥ 2). Consider an arbitrary w such that $|w| = t$.

Clearly, (i) w is in L_i if and only if (ii) a production $A_i \rightarrow bA_j$ is in P and $w = bw_1$ where w_1 is in L_j, or else (ii)$'$ a production $A_i \rightarrow bA_jA_k$ is in P and w can be written as $w = bw_2w_3$ where w_2 is in L_j and w_3 is in L_k.

By the definition of σ and by the inductive hypothesis, (ii) holds if and only if (iii) $\sigma(b)$ contains the word $\bar{a}_1 \bar{a}_2^i \bar{a}_1 a_1 a_2^j a_1$ and $\sigma(w_1)$ contains a word $\bar{a}_1 \bar{a}_2^j \bar{a}_1 x_1$ where $w = bw_1$ and $x_1 \in D_2$. Similarly, (ii)$'$ holds if and only if (iii)$'$ $\sigma(b)$ contains the word

$$\bar{a}_1 \bar{a}_2^i \bar{a}_1 a_1 a_2^k a_1 a_1 a_2^j a_1,$$

$\sigma(w_2)$ contains a word $\bar{a}_1 \bar{a}_2^j \bar{a}_1 x_2$ and $\sigma(w_3)$ contains a word $\bar{a}_1 \bar{a}_2^k \bar{a}_1 x_3$, where $w = bw_2w_3$, and x_2 and x_3 are in D_2.

To complete the inductive step, we now show that (iv) $\sigma(w)$ contains a word in (6.15) if and only if (iii) or (iii)$'$ holds. This shows that the conditions (i) and (iv) are equivalent, which is exactly what we want.

It is an immediate consequence of the definition of D_2 that if (iii) or (iii)$'$ holds then also (iv) holds. Conversely, assume that (iv) holds, i.e., $\sigma(w)$ contains a word

$$y = \bar{a}_1 \bar{a}_2^i \bar{a}_1 x, \quad x \in D_2. \tag{6.17}$$

We write $w = bw_1$, where b is a letter. Hence,

$$y = y_1 y_2, \quad y_1 \in \sigma(b), \quad y_2 \in \sigma(w_1). \tag{6.18}$$

Recall that $|w| \geq 2$ and, consequently, $w_1 \neq \lambda$. Hence, $x \neq \lambda$. We cannot have $y_1 = \bar{a}_1 \bar{a}_2^i \bar{a}_1$ because this would imply that the word $x = y_2$ both belongs to D_2 and begins with barred letters (because it is in $\sigma(w_1)$), two conditions which cannot be satisfied simultaneously. Hence, by (6.14), we have either

$$y_1 = \bar{a}_1 \bar{a}_2{}^i \bar{a}_1 a_1 a_2{}^j a_1, \tag{6.19}$$

or else

$$y_1 = \bar{a}_1 \bar{a}_2{}^i \bar{a}_1 a_1 a_2{}^k a_1 a_1 a_2{}^j a_1. \tag{6.20}$$

It suffices to show that (6.19) (resp. (6.20)) implies (iii) (resp. (iii)').
  Assume (6.19). We claim that

$$y_2 = \bar{a}_1 \bar{a}_2{}^j \bar{a}_1 x_1, \tag{6.21}$$

which by (6.17)–(6.19) shows the validity of (iii). Indeed, if (6.21) does not hold then

$$y_2 = \bar{a}_1 \bar{a}_2{}^p \bar{a}_1 y_2', \qquad p \neq j,$$

and

$$x = a_1 a_2{}^j a_1 \bar{a}_1 \bar{a}_2{}^p \bar{a}_1 y_2'.$$

Clearly, this gives the result $\rho(x) \neq \lambda$ for the Dyck mapping ρ, independently of y_2'. This contradiction with (6.17) shows that (6.21) holds.
  Assume, finally, that (6.20) holds. In this case we claim that

$$y_2 = \bar{a}_1 \bar{a}_2{}^j \bar{a}_1 x_2 \bar{a}_1 \bar{a}_2{}^k \bar{a}_1 x_3, \tag{6.22}$$

for some x_2 and x_3 in D_2, where

$$\bar{a}_1 \bar{a}_2{}^j \bar{a}_1 x_2 \in \sigma(w_2), \, \bar{a}_1 \bar{a}_2{}^k \bar{a}_1 x_3 \in \sigma(w_3), \, w_1 = w_2 w_3. \tag{6.23}$$

Clearly, (6.20), (6.22) and (6.23) show the validity of (iii)'.
  The relations (6.22) and (6.23) are consequences of the following observations. The word y_2 must begin with $\bar{a}_1 \bar{a}_2{}^j \bar{a}_1$; this is seen exactly as in (6.21). The word y_2 is obtained by catenating words of the form $a_1 a_2{}^p a_1$ and $\bar{a}_1 \bar{a}_2{}^p \bar{a}_1$, $p = 1, \ldots, n$. By (6.20), y_2 must contain also (after $\bar{a}_1 \bar{a}_2{}^j \bar{a}_1$) the subword $\bar{a}_1 \bar{a}_2{}^k \bar{a}_1$ because, otherwise, we cannot have $\rho(x) = \lambda$. Thus, we obtain (6.22) and, by considering ρ again, we see that $x_2, x_3 \in D_2$. Because x_2 and x_3 are in

D_2 and, hence, (if nonempty) must end with barred letters, we obtain a decomposition $w_1 = w_2 w_3$ satisfying (6.23).   □

The morphic generator of context-free languages, referred to at the beginning of this section, is now easily obtainable from Theorem 6.5. We only change the definition (6.14) to make σ a morphism. This is done simply by catenating the words on the right side, after separating them by boundary markers. We use the symbol "+" for the boundary marker to remind us that we are dealing with a "sum" of words. The generator language D has to be modified to allow space for the "garbage" coming from the productions unused at each step.

We now give the formal details. As before, Σ is the alphabet $\{a_1, a_2, \bar{a}_1, \bar{a}_2\}$. The language L_0 over the alphabet

$$\Sigma_1 = \Sigma \cup \{+\}$$

is defined by

$$L_0 = \{x_1 + y_1 + z_1 x_2 + y_2 + z_2 \cdots x_t + y_t + z_t \mid t \geq 1,$$
$$y_1 y_2 \cdots y_t \in D, y_i \neq \lambda, x_i \in (+\Sigma^+)^*, z_i \in (\Sigma^+ +)^*, \quad \text{for } 1 \leq i \leq t\}.$$

It is easy to show that L_0 is context-free, cf. Exercise 6.

Given an arbitrary λ-free context-free language L as in the proof of Theorem 6.5, we define a morphism

$$h : \Sigma_L^* \rightarrow \Sigma_1^*$$

as follows. Consider an arbitrary letter b in Σ_L. Let

$$\{\alpha_1, \ldots, \alpha_u\}$$

be the set of words appearing on the right side of (6.14). Then define

$$h(b) = +\alpha_1 + \alpha_2 + \cdots + \alpha_u + . \tag{6.24}$$

The following lemma establishes the interconnection between σ and h.

Lemma 6.6.   For every word w over Σ_L, $h(w)$ belongs to L_0 if and only if $\sigma(w)$ has a word in common with D.

Proof.   The words in L_0 are of the form

$$\cdots + y_1 + \cdots + + \cdots + y_2 + \cdots + + \cdots + + \cdots + y_t + \cdots ,$$
$$y_1 y_2 \cdots y_t \in D, \qquad (6.25)$$

where the indicated $t - 1$ occurrences of the subword $+ +$ are the only ones in the whole word. Because in (6.24) the α's are nonempty words over Σ, the subword $+ +$ does not occur in any $h(b)$.

The lemma clearly holds for $w = \lambda$. Consider $w = b_1 \cdots b_t$, $t \geq 1$. Assume first that $h(w)$ is in L_0. We write $h(w)$ in the form (6.25). Then, by (6.24), the subwords $+ +$ occur exactly on the border between $h(b_i)$ and $h(b_{i+1})$, for $i = 1, \ldots, t - 1$. By (6.24), $y_i \in \sigma(b_i)$, $i = 1, \ldots, t$, which shows that the word $y_1 \cdots y_t \in D$ is also in $\sigma(w)$.

Conversely, if $\sigma(b_i)$ contains a word y_i, for $i = 1, \ldots, t$, such that $y_1 \cdots y_t \in D$, we conclude by (6.24) that $h(w)$ can be written in the form (6.25), showing that $h(w)$ is in L_0. Observe that we have taken care of the possibility that y_i appears as the first or last item in (6.24), because in the definition of L_0 we allow $x_i = \lambda$ and $z_i = \lambda$. $\square$

We want to emphasize that the expression (6.25) for a word $h(w)$ in L_0 is by no means unique: such an expression may be valid for different y's. This reflects the fact that the word w can have several derivations according to G, a point further exploited in Exercise 8.

Theorem 6.5 and Lemma 6.6 show that

$$L = h^{-1}(L_0).$$

Hence, we have established the following fundamental result to the effect that L_0 is a "morphic generator" for context-free languages. As in connection with Theorem 6.5, the assumption concerning λ-freeness is not essential: $L_0 \cup \{\lambda\}$ can be used in the same way as a generator for context-free languages containing λ. (Clearly, no single language generates both of these language classes.)

Theorem 6.7.   For every λ-free context-free language L, there is a morphism h such that

$$L = h^{-1}(L_0).$$

6.3 GENERATION OF RECURSIVELY ENUMERABLE LANGUAGES BY MORPHISMS

That a result corresponding to Theorem 6.7 holds also for the family of recursively enumerable languages follows by the very essence of this family. Indeed every language, the words of which can be listed by some effective procedure ("effective" in the intuitive sense), is also generated by a type 0 grammar. This statement (generally referred to as "Church's thesis") will be used in our next proof although the proof can be also carried out without it, cf. Exercise 10. The reader is referred to [Sa 2] for a further discussion concerning Church's thesis.

Theorem 6.8.   There is a type 0 language L_0 with the following property. For every λ-free type 0 language L, there is a morphism h such that $L = h^{-1}(L_0)$.

Proof.   We may consider without loss of generality type 0 languages generated by a grammar whose nonterminal (resp. terminal) alphabet is a finite initial segment of the infinite set

$$\{S_1, S_2, S_3, \ldots\}, (\text{resp. } \{b_1, b_2, b_3, \ldots\}), \tag{6.26}$$

and where S_1 is the only start symbol. Let

$$G_1, G_2, \ldots$$

be an enumeration of all these grammars, based on the total number of occurrences of letters in the productions. To each of the grammars G_i we associate a word of the form

$$\# p_1 \# p_2 \# \cdots \# p_k \#, \tag{6.27}$$

where $p_1, \ldots, p_k$ are the productions of G_i. Thus, words of the form (6.27) contain two special letters $\#$ and $\rightarrow$ and, in addition, letters from (6.26). All of these letters are now encoded using the alphabet $\{a_1, a_2\}$. (For instance, we represent all letters in the form $a_1 a_2^i a_1$. The values $i = 1, 2$ are reserved for the special letters and, otherwise, odd and even values of i are used to encode nonterminals and terminals, respectively.) When this encoding is applied to (6.27), we obtain a word

$$s(G_i) \in \{a_1, a_2\}^+$$

associated to G_i.

For $i \geq 1$, we define now a morphism $h_i : \Sigma_i^* \to \{a_1, a_2\}^*$, where Σ_i is the terminal alphabet of G_i, as follows. Let $b \in \Sigma_i$ be arbitrary and let $e(b)$ be its encoding (as defined above) in terms of a_1 and a_2. Define

$$h_i(b) = s(G_i)\, e(b).$$

Define, finally,

$$L_0 = \bigcup_{i=1}^{\infty} h_i(L(G_i)) \backslash \{\lambda\}.$$

The language L_0 can be listed effectively, for instance, by a procedure whose nth step consists of listing all nonempty words generated according to some of the grammars $G_1, \ldots, G_n$ by a derivation of length $\leq n$. Thus, by Church's thesis, L_0 is of type 0.

On the other hand, if $L = L(G_i)$ and $\lambda \notin L$, then $L = h_i^{-1}(L_0)$. This result follows immediately because the "signature" $s(G_i)$ appears in those words of L_0 only that come from $L(G_i)$.   □

Observe that if $\lambda \in L$, then $h_i^{-1}(L_0)$ equals the language $L\backslash\{\lambda\}$. It is not possible to tell in advance which of the languages $L(G_i)$ are λ-free. In fact, it is undecidable to determine whether λ belongs to a given $L(G_i)$.

As we have already pointed out, Theorem 6.8 is due to the universal nature of type 0 grammars. We shall now discuss some more specific morphic representations for type 0 languages. It turns out that equality sets are very useful for such representations.

We want to represent an arbitrary recursively enumerable language as a morphic image of an equality set. This result would be a representation of all recursively enumerable languages entirely in terms of morphisms! As such, this requirement is a little too strong because of the following reason. Every equality language is a "star language," i.e., of the form $L = L_1^*$ and, hence, the same is true of languages $h(L)$. However, if we allow a suitable mechanism for selecting a subset of the equality language, then such a morphic representation is indeed possible. A very simple mechanism suitable for this purpose is to intersect the equality language with a regular language. This mechanism is quite widely used in various parts of language theory. Another possible way of overcoming the difficulty is given in Exercise 11.

If Σ and Σ_1, $\Sigma \subseteq \Sigma_1$, are alphabets, the morphism $H_\Sigma : \Sigma_1^* \to \Sigma^*$ is defined by

$$H_\Sigma(a) = \begin{cases} a \text{ for } a \in \Sigma, \\ \lambda \text{ for } a \in \Sigma_1 \backslash \Sigma. \end{cases}$$

Thus, H_Σ erases everything except the letters in Σ.

Theorem 6.9. For every recursively enumerable language $L \subseteq \Sigma_T{}^*$, there are two morphisms h_1 and h_2 and a regular language R such that

$$L = H_{\Sigma_T}(E(h_1, h_2) \cap R). \tag{6.28}$$

Proof. Consider an arbitrary recursively enumerable language L, generated by a type 0 grammar G, where Σ_N and Σ_T are the nonterminal and terminal alphabets, $S \in \Sigma_N$ is the start letter, and the production set P consists of productions

$$p_i : \alpha_i \rightarrow \beta_i, \; i = 1, \ldots, n.$$

(Thus, we associate a name p_i to each production.)

Essentially, the idea behind the construction of h_1, h_2 and R is the following. Every word in L appears as the last word in some derivation D according to G. For a word D' resembling D, the morphisms h_1 and h_2 satisfy

$$h_1(D') = h_2(D').$$

However, h_1 "runs faster" than h_2 on prefixes of D', and h_2 "catches up" only at the end. The morphism H_Σ erases everything else except the end result. Finally, R is used to insure that only words of the proper form are taken into account.

We now give the formal details. We use "primed versions" of alphabets in the same way as before: Σ' is the alphabet $\{a' | a \in \Sigma\}$, and w' is a word obtained from w by providing every letter with a prime. We shall consider the alphabets

$$\Sigma_1 = \Sigma_N \cup \Sigma_T \cup \{\#\},$$
$$\Sigma_2 = \Sigma_1 \cup P \cup \Sigma_T{}' \cup \{B, F\}.$$

The morphisms $h_1, h_2 : \Sigma_2{}^* \rightarrow \Sigma_1{}^*$ are defined by the table

	B	$\#$	$p_i \in P \; (p_i : \alpha_i \rightarrow \beta_i)$	$A \in \Sigma_N$	$a' \in \Sigma_T{}'$	$a \in \Sigma_T$	F
h_1	$S\#$	$\#$	β_i	A	a	λ	λ
h_2	λ	$\#$	α_i	A	a	a	$\#$

Furthermore, we define the regular language R by the regular expression

$$B(V_1^* PV_1^* \#)^+ \Sigma_T^* F \quad \text{where} \quad V_1 = \Sigma_N \cup \Sigma_T'.$$

We still have to show that (6.28) holds. We first take an example. Consider a grammar with the productions

$$p_1 : S \to ACCC, p_2 : CC \to CD, p_3 : AC \to a,$$
$$p_4 : DC \to ACC, p_5 : AC \to \lambda, p_6 : C \to b.$$

The word ab is in the language of this grammar, as seen from the derivation

$$S \Rightarrow ACCC \Rightarrow ACDC \Rightarrow aDC \Rightarrow aACC \Rightarrow aC \Rightarrow ab. \quad (6.29)$$

With this derivation we now associate the word

$$w = Bp_1 \# Ap_2 C \# p_3 DC \# a\,'p_4 \# a\,'p_5 C \# a\,'p_6 \# abF$$

and observe that $H_{\{a,b\}}(w) = ab$ and that w is in R. Furthermore, $h_1(w) = h_2(w)$, both sides being equal to the word obtained from (6.29) by replacing $\Rightarrow$ with $\#$ and adding one further occurrence of $\#$ to the end.

Returning to the proof, we first show that an arbitrary word $x \in L$ belongs also to the right side of (6.28). To do this, we need only to establish inductively the following assertion: Whenever

$$S \Rightarrow \alpha_1 \Rightarrow \alpha_2 \Rightarrow \cdots \Rightarrow \alpha_k \quad (6.30)$$

is a derivation according to G, there is a word $w \in B(V_1^* PV_1^* \#)^+$ such that

$$h_1(w) = S \# \alpha_1 \# \alpha_2 \# \cdots \# \alpha_k \#,$$
$$h_2(w) = S \# \alpha_1 \# \alpha_2 \# \cdots \# \alpha_{k-1} \# .$$

This is clearly sufficient because if $\alpha_k = x$ is a terminal word, then

$$wxF \in E(h_1, h_2) \cap R \quad \text{and} \quad H_{\Sigma_T}(wxF) = x.$$

For $k = 1$, we may choose $w = Bp_1 \#$, where p_1 is the name of the production $S \to \alpha_1$. As an inductive hypothesis, assume the assertion holds true for the value k. Thus, for an arbitrary derivation (6.30), there is a word w satisfying the required conditions. We continue (6.30) with an additional step

$$\alpha_k \Rightarrow \alpha_{k+1}, \quad \text{where} \quad \alpha_k = \beta_1 \alpha \beta_2, \; \alpha_{k+1} = \beta_1 \beta \beta_2$$

and the production $p : \alpha \to \beta$ is in P. Let β_1' (resp. β_2') be the word obtained from β_1 (resp. β_2) by providing all terminals with primes (and leaving nonterminals unchanged). Then the word $w\beta_1'p\beta_2'\#$ satisfies the required conditions for the longer derivation. This completes the inductive step.

Conversely, consider an arbitrary word

$$x = H_{\Sigma_T}(w) \quad \text{where} \quad w \in E(h_1, h_2) \cap R.$$

Since w is in R, we may write it in the form

$$w = Bw_1 \cdots w_k \, xF \quad \text{where} \quad w_i \in V_1^* \, PV_1^*\#, \; 1 \le i \le k.$$

Observe, in particular, that the word x must appear before F because $x = H_{\Sigma_T}(w)$ and all letters not belonging to Σ_T are erased by H_{Σ_T}.

We now make use of the fact that $h_1(w) = h_2(w)$. If $\overline{w}$ is a prefix of w, then one of $h_1(\overline{w})$ and $h_2(\overline{w})$ must be a prefix of the other. The situation is easy to handle by looking at occurrences of $\#$. The letter B introduces one occurrence of $\#$ to the h_1-image but none to the h_2-image. Each of the words w_i introduces one occurrence of $\#$ to the end of both the h_1-image and h_2-image. Consequently, h_1 "runs faster," i.e., $h_2(\overline{w})$ is a prefix of $h_1(\overline{w})$.

In particular, we have

$$h_1(Bw_1 \cdots w_k) = S \# w_1^{(1)} \# w_2^{(1)} \# \cdots \# w_k^{(1)} \#,$$

for some words $w_i^{(1)}$, and consequently

$$h_2(Bw_1 \cdots w_k) = S \# w_1^{(1)} \# w_2^{(1)} \# \cdots \# w_{k-1}^{(1)} \#.$$

Because h_2 still "catches up" h_1 when mapping xF, we must have $w_k^{(1)} = x$.

For $i = 1, \ldots, k$, the word w_i "deposits" the word $w_i^{(1)} \#$ to the h_1-image and the word $w_{i-1}^{(1)} \#$ to the h_2-image. (Here we denote $w_0^{(1)} = S$.) This implies, because w_i is in $V_1^* \, PV_1^* \#$, that we may write

$$w_{i-1}^{(1)} = \beta_1 \alpha \beta_2, \; w_i^{(1)} = \beta_1 \beta \beta_2,$$

where $\alpha \to \beta$ is a production in P. But this means that we have a derivation

$$S \Rightarrow w_1^{(1)} \Rightarrow w_2^{(1)} \Rightarrow \cdots \Rightarrow w_k^{(1)}$$

with $w_k^{(1)} = x$ and, consequently, x is in L.   □

Theorem 6.9 can be used also to characterize type 0 languages in terms of an especially simple generator. Such a generator, called a *twin-shuffle language*, will now be defined.

Consider an alphabet Σ, as well as the barred version $\overline{\Sigma}$. (Similarly as with primes, $\overline{\Sigma} = \{\overline{a} | a \in \Sigma\}$. The notation $\overline{w}$ indicates that all letters of w have been barred.) The twin-shuffle language L_Σ is defined as follows:

$$L_\Sigma = \{w \in (\Sigma \cup \overline{\Sigma})^* | \overline{H_\Sigma(w)} = H_{\overline{\Sigma}}(w)\}.$$

Thus, L_Σ consists of words obtained by taking an arbitrary word $x \in \Sigma^*$, its barred version $\overline{x}$, and "shuffling" the two in an arbitrary fashion. If the morphism

$$h : (\Sigma \cup \overline{\Sigma})^* \to \Sigma^*$$

is defined by

$$h(a) = \begin{cases} \lambda \text{ for } a \in \Sigma, \\ b \text{ for } a = \overline{b} \in \overline{\Sigma}, \end{cases}$$

then clearly $L_\Sigma = E(h, H_\Sigma)$.

Theorem 6.10. For every recursively enumerable language $L \subseteq \Sigma_T^*$, there is a twin-shuffle language L_Σ and a regular language R_1 such that

$$L = H_{\Sigma_T}(L_\Sigma \cap R_1). \tag{6.31}$$

Proof. Consider the representation (6.28) given in Theorem 6.9. We may assume that Σ_2 and Σ_1, i.e., the range and target alphabets of h_1 and h_2, are disjoint. (To accomplish this purpose, we simply rename the letters of Σ_1; this new designation has no influence on (6.28).)

Define now $\Sigma = \Sigma_2 \cup \Sigma_1$. Let g be the morphism satisfying

$$g(b) = bh_1(b) \, \overline{h_2(b)} \quad \text{for every} \quad b \in \Sigma_2.$$

Finally, let R_1 be the language obtained from the language $g(R)$ by inserting to its words letters of $\overline{\Sigma_2}$ in an arbitrary fashion. Thus, R_1 consists of words of the form

$$x_1 b_1 x_2 b_2 \cdots x_k b_k x_{k+1}, x_1 x_2 \cdots x_{k+1} \in g(R),$$

where b's are letters from $\overline{\Sigma}_2$ and x's are words (possibly empty). Clearly, R_1 is regular.

The equation (6.31) is now a direct consequence of (6.28) and the relation

$$H_{\Sigma_T}(L_\Sigma \cap R_1) = H_{\Sigma_T}(E(h_1, h_2) \cap R),$$

the latter being immediate by the definitions.   □

In Theorem 6.10, the alphabet Σ depends on the language L. This relationship is not essential: some stronger versions of the result are given in Exercises 3 and 14.

The results in this chapter show that twin-shuffle languages and Dyck languages play a similar role in the theories of type 0 and context-free languages, respectively. In conclusion, we mention without proof the following rather peculiar representation theorem. A proof is outlined in Exercise 15. The symbols ρ and D denote the Dyck mapping and the initialized Dyck language, as defined above. As regards ρ, we allow a superset of the original alphabet $\Sigma_1 \cup \overline{\Sigma}_1$. The additional symbols in this superset are unaffected by ρ.

Theorem 6.11.   For every recursively enumerable language $L \subseteq \Sigma_T{}^+$, there is a morphism h such that

$$L = \rho(h^{-1}(D)) \cap \Sigma_T*.$$

EXERCISES

1. Prove that every regular language R can be expressed in the form $R = h(L)$, where L is local and the morphism h maps every letter either to a letter or to the empty word. (Thus, no assumptions are made about the empty word being or not being in R.)

2. Theorems 6.7 and 6.8 exhibit the generative capacity of inverse morphisms. Morphisms are much weaker in this respect: intuitively, no "hiding" is possible when morphisms are considered. Prove that there is no type 0 language L_0 such that every type 0 language is of the form $h(L_0)$. Prove also the analogous result for context-free languages. These results are valid even if finite substitutions are considered instead of morphisms.

3. The generative capacity of morphisms increases considerably if one considers the operator of intersecting with a regular language also. Theorem 6.10 shows that every recursively enumerable language is a morphic image of the intersection between a twin-shuffle language and a regular language. Prove the analogous

result for context-free languages: every context-free language equals a morphic image of the intersection between a Dyck language and a regular language. (This result is known as the Chomsky-Schützenberger theorem.) In these results, no single twin-shuffle or Dyck language is sufficient. Prove, however, that for all context-free (resp. type 0) languages over the same alphabet Σ_T, one fixed Dyck (resp. twin-shuffle) language is sufficient.

4. Generalize Lemmas 6.3 and 6.4 to the following "super normal form" theorem. Assume that (m, n, p) is an arbitrary triple of nonnegative integers. Then every context-free language is generated by a grammar whose productions are of the following two forms:

    (i) $A \rightarrow w$ where w is a terminal word,
    (ii) $A \rightarrow w_m B w_n C w_p$, where w_m, w_n, w_p are terminal words of lengths m, n, p, respectively.

    (Lemma 6.3 gives essentially this result for the triple $(0,0,0)$, and Lemma 6.4 for the triple $(1,0,0)$.) Cf. [MSW 1]. Can you strengthen (i) in such a way that $|w|$ is always in the length set of the language considered? The length set of a language consists of all lengths of the words in the language.

5. Go through the induction in the proof of Theorem 6.5 by choosing $t = 0$ as the basis. (The inductive step will be slightly more involved than with the basis $t = 1$.)

6. Prove that the language L_0 defined before Lemma 6.6 is context-free. (Hint. Generate first D as before but viewing terminals as special nonterminals. Give productions for these special nonterminals, allowing them to terminate either directly or after pushing a word of a proper form to the left and/or to the right.)

7. Consider the context-free language generated by the grammar G:

    $$S \rightarrow a, \ S \rightarrow bS, \ S \rightarrow cS^2.$$

    (This language L is known as the Lukasiewicz language.) Give for L representations according to Theorems 6.5 and 6.7. Study, in particular, how derivations according to G are reflected in the morphism h. Cf. [SalS].

8. Study the interconnection between the number of different expressions (6.25) for $h(w)$ and the "ambiguity" of w in G, i.e., the number of different derivations of w according to G.

9. (For an algebraically minded reader.) Consider the Dyck mapping ρ. Define in Σ^* the congruence E_ρ by

    $$w E_\rho w_1 \quad \text{if and only if} \quad \rho(w) = \rho(w_1).$$

    Then the factor monoid Σ^*/E_ρ is known as the *involutive monoid*. If both-sided cancellations are allowed, i.e., if we have $\bar{a}_i a_i = \lambda$ in addition to $a_i \bar{a}_i = \lambda$, then we obtain similarly the free group generated by Σ_1, as well as the corresponding languages $\overline{D}_k$, consisting of words reducible to λ by the both-sided cancellations. Give representation results analogous to Theorems 6.5 and 6.7, starting with $\overline{D}_2$ instead of D_2. (These results can be viewed as representations in terms of free groups instead of involutive monoids.)

10. Prove that the language L_0 in the proof of Theorem 6.8 is of type 0, without using Church's thesis. (It is a very tedious task to construct the type 0 grammar explicitly. Instead, convince yourself that this can be done. Observe, in particular, that derivations can be carried out between two boundary markers, and "messengers" can be sent from one marker to the other. In this way, the derivation can be divided into stages in such a way that a new stage is never begun before some condition, showing the termination of the previous stage, is satisfied.)

11. Denote by $e(h_1, h_2)$ the subset of $E(h_1, h_2)$ consisting of all nonempty words w such that no proper prefix of w (i.e., a prefix $\neq w$, λ) is in $E(h_1, h_2)$. Prove that every recursively enumerable language over Σ_T can be represented in the form $H_{\Sigma_T}(e(h_1, h_2))$. Cf. [Cu].

12. Consider the sets $E_k(h_1, h_2)$ defined in Exercise 4.8. Prove that a language L is regular if and only if there are morphisms g, h_1, h_2 such that $L = g(e(h_1, h_2))$ and, moreover,

$$e(h_1, h_2) \subseteq E_k(h_1, h_2), \quad \text{for some} \quad k.$$

Cf. [Cu].

13. We say that a language L is an *equality language* if it is of the form

$$L = E(h_1, h_2),$$

for some h_1 and h_2. Show that the family of equality languages is the smallest family containing L_Σ with $\Sigma = \{a, b\}$ and closed under inverse morphisms. Cf. [EnR].

14. Strengthen Theorem 6.10 to the following form. For every recursively enumerable language L over Σ_T, there is a morphism g and a regular language R such that

$$L = H_{\Sigma_T}(g^{-1}(L_{\{a,b\}}) \cap R).$$

15. Establish Theorem 6.11. (Hints. Prove first that every λ-free type 0 language is generated by a grammar with productions of the forms $A \rightarrow BC$, $AB \rightarrow C$, $A \rightarrow a$. Consider such a grammar. Introduce for each nonterminal A two new letters y_A and $\bar{y}_A$. Replace each production $AB \rightarrow C$ with the production $A \rightarrow Cy_B$. Add all productions $A \rightarrow \bar{y}_A$. Apply Theorem 6.7.)

Chapter 7

LANGUAGE FAMILIES

7.1 REGULAR LANGUAGES AS A GRAMMATICAL FAMILY

We have met so far several families of languages. However, the attention has been focused on specific families; no general theory of language families has been developed. Such a theory can be based on closure properties: one investigates language families closed under certain specified operations. Some further facts and a reference concerning this approach are given in Exercises 1 and 2. Following the central theme of this book, we shall now study a theory of language families, based on morphisms. Roughly speaking, this approach means the following.

Starting with a fixed grammar G, "master grammar," we consider inverse morphic images of G (in a sense to be made precise below). They can be viewed as grammars "similar" to G. Each of the inverse morphic images generates a language. We can now associate with an arbitrary master grammar G a family of languages, namely, the languages generated by inverse morphic images of G. In this chapter we shall be concerned with such language families, referred to as *grammatical* families. The attention will be restricted to context-free master grammars.

We shall find some of our old friends, such as the families of regular and context-free languages, among the grammatical families so defined. Since parallel rewriting is essentially different, we do not find the families of DOL or OL languages among them. It is possible to develop an analogous definitional mechanism to take care of the L families, cf. [RS] or [W].

Apart from providing a natural model for the similarity of grammars, the theory of master grammars and grammatical families is also a natural way of studying all possible normal forms for grammars generating some specific language family. Examples of this process will be given below. We shall also exhibit a method of constructing "many" grammatical families, in fact even dense hierarchies of them. Finally, we shall show how a special case of this theory is closely linked with colorings of graphs.

We shall now begin the formal details.

Consider a grammar G with the set P of productions, nonterminal and terminal alphabets Σ_N and Σ_T, and $\Sigma_S \subseteq \Sigma_N$ as the set of start symbols. Let

$$h : \Sigma_N^* \to V_N^*, \quad h : \Sigma_T^* \to V_T^*$$

be a letter-to-letter morphism. Assume, further, that every letter of $V_N \cup V_T$ appears as an h-image. Thus, the cardinality of V_N (resp. V_T) equals at most that of Σ_N (resp. Σ_T), and we may write

$$h(\Sigma_N) = V_N \text{ and } h(\Sigma_T) = V_T.$$

The set $h(P)$ is defined in the natural way by

$$h(P) = \{h(\alpha) \to h(\beta) | \alpha \to \beta \text{ in } P\}.$$

Observe now that $G_1 = (V_N, V_T, h(P), h(\Sigma_S))$ is also a grammar. We call G_1 a *morphic image* of G and denote

$$G_1 = h(G). \tag{7.1}$$

The requirement of h being letter-to-letter is essential because, otherwise, we do not obtain proper alphabets for the new grammar G_1.

A grammar $G = (\Sigma_N, \Sigma_T, P, \Sigma_S)$ is a *subgrammar* of a grammar $G' = (\Sigma_N', \Sigma_T', P', \Sigma_S')$ if $\Sigma_N \subseteq \Sigma_N'$, $\Sigma_S \subseteq \Sigma_S'$, $\Sigma_T \subseteq \Sigma_T'$ and $P \subseteq P'$.

A grammar G is said to be an *inverse morphic image* of a grammar G_1' if (7.1) is satisfied for some letter-to-letter morphism h and a subgrammar G_1 of G_1'. The fact that G is an inverse morphic image of G_1' under a (letter-to-letter) morphism h is denoted by

$$G \in h^{-1}(G_1'). \tag{7.2}$$

The reader might wonder why (7.1) and (7.2) are not symmetric. A "super-grammar" G_1' of G_1 is used in (7.2) to provide more leeway: a grammar is an inverse morphic image of another grammar if the former can be mapped morphically onto a subgrammar of the latter. This is quite essential: we want to be able to use only a subset of the production set. Further information is given in Exercise 3.

The *language family* generated by a grammar G is defined by

$$\mathcal{L}(G) = \{L(G_1) | G_1 \in h^{-1}(G) \text{ for some } h\}.$$

A family $\mathcal{L}$ of languages is termed *grammatical* if $\mathcal{L} = \mathcal{L}(G)$, for some G. If, in addition, G is a context-free grammar then $\mathcal{L}(G)$ is termed a context-free grammatical family. All grammatical families and grammars discussed in this chapter will be context-free, even if this is not explicitly mentioned.

To avoid unnecessary special cases, we consider only λ-free languages in this chapter. When speaking of specific language families, such as the families of regular and context-free languages, we mean the collection of λ-free languages in these families.

As an example, consider the grammar determined by the productions

$$S \to SS, \quad S \to a. \tag{7.3}$$

It is an immediate consequence of Lemma 6.3 that the language family generated by this grammar is the family of context-free languages. Similarly, it follows by Lemma 2.2 that the family generated by the grammar

$$S \to aS, \quad S \to a, \tag{7.4}$$

is the family of regular languages.

Two grammars G_1 and G_2 are called *family equivalent* if $\mathcal{L}(G_1) = \mathcal{L}(G_2)$. (Recall that G_1 and G_2 are equivalent if $L(G_1) = L(G_2)$.) Clearly, two grammars can be family equivalent without being equivalent, and vice versa. For instance, (7.3) and (7.4) are equivalent (both generate the language a^+) but not family equivalent. On the other hand, a renaming of the terminal alphabet of a grammar G (such as providing all terminals with primes) leaves the family $\mathcal{L}(G)$ invariant, whereas it changes $L(G)$ (apart from the trivial case where $L(G)$ does not contain any nonempty words).

A grammar is called *regular-complete* (resp. *regular-sufficient*) if its language family equals (resp. contains) the family of regular languages. Thus, both (7.3) and (7.4) are regular-sufficient and (7.4) is, in addition, regular-complete. A grammar is called *context-free-complete* or, briefly, *complete* if its language family equals the family of context-free languages. (Recall that we are considering only context-free grammars. Since morphisms and inverse morphisms preserve context-freeness, the largest family generated by a grammar is the family of context-free languages. Thus, it does not make sense to talk about context-free-sufficiency!) The grammar (7.3) is complete.

The notions of completeness and sufficiency can be defined for other language families as well. Observe that each complete grammar gives a "normal form" for context-free grammars. Thus (7.3) gives the Chomsky normal form of Lemma 6.3. Consequently, a characterization of completeness is at the same time a characterization of all possible normal forms for context-free grammars. The same holds true with respect to other families as well: a characterization of regular-completeness is at the same time a characterization of all possible normal forms for grammars for regular languages. Such a characterization is given below.

In the literature inverse morphic images of grammars are often called *interpretations*. Moreover when language families, rather than languages, generated by grammars are discussed, then the grammars are often referred to as *grammar forms*. The inverse morphism can be replaced by the direct operation of a finite substitution as follows. Consider a grammar $G = (\Sigma_N, \Sigma_T, P, \Sigma_S)$ and let σ be a finite substitution, defined on the alphabet $\Sigma_N \cup \Sigma_T$, such that $\sigma(a)$ is a finite (possibly empty) set of letters for each letter a, and $a \neq b$ always implies $\sigma(a) \cap \sigma(b) = \phi$. Denote

$$\sigma(\Sigma_N) = \Sigma_N', \quad \sigma(\Sigma_T) = \Sigma_T'.$$

Let Σ_S' be a subset of $\sigma(\Sigma_S)$, and P' a subset of $\sigma(P)$ (where the latter is defined in the natural fashion). Then the grammar

$$G' = (\Sigma_N', \Sigma_T', P', \Sigma_S')$$

is said to be an *interpretation* of G. It is immediate that this notion of an interpretation coincides with the above one, i.e., with the notion of an inverse morphic image. The set of all interpretations of G is denoted by $\mathfrak{M}(G)$.

The following three lemmas are immediate from the definitions. The proofs are, therefore, omitted.

Lemma 7.1. There is an algorithm for deciding of two given grammars G and G_1 whether or not G_1 is an interpretation of G. If G_1 is an interpretation of G and G_2 an interpretation of G_1, then also G_2 is an interpretation of G. Consequently, if G_1 is an interpretation G, then the language family generated by G_1 is contained in that generated by G.

Lemma 7.2. For every language L in $\mathcal{L}(G)$, there is a letter-to-letter morphism h such that $h(L) \subseteq L(G)$. Consequently, the length set of every language in $\mathcal{L}(G)$ is contained in the length set of $L(G)$.

Lemma 7.3. The language $L(G)$ is finite if and only if every language in $\mathcal{L}(G)$ is finite. If

$$L(G) = \{w_1, \ldots, w_n\}$$

is finite, then G is family equivalent to the grammar determined by the productions

$$S \to w_1, \ldots, S \to w_n.$$

We shall now deduce characterizations for regular-completeness and regular-sufficiency. First we need two definitions.

Let a be a letter in the terminal alphabet of a grammar G (context-free, as agreed above). The *a-restriction* G_a of G is obtained from G by removing all terminals $\neq a$ and all productions involving some of them.

A grammar G is *self-embedding* if it has a derivation

$$S \Rightarrow {}^* w_1 A w_2 \Rightarrow {}^* w_1 w_3 A w_4 w_2 \Rightarrow {}^* w_1 w_3 w_5 w_4 w_2, \tag{7.5}$$

where $S \in \Sigma_S$, the w's are terminal words and $w_3 \neq \lambda$, $w_4 \neq \lambda$.

Lemma 7.4.   The language family of a grammar G contains a non-regular language if and only if G is self-embedding.

Proof.   Assume that G is self-embedding. We consider a derivation (7.5). By isolating the productions used in this derivation and by taking primed versions of the letters appearing in w_4, we obtain an interpretation G_1 of G such that

$$L(G_1) = \{w_1 w_3{}^n w_5 (w_4{}')^n w_2 \,|\, n \geq 0\}.$$

Clearly, $L(G_1)$ is non-regular and, consequently, $\mathcal{L}(G)$ contains a non-regular language.

Conversely, assume that G is not self-embedding. If some interpretation G_1 of G has a derivation (7.5), we consider the letter-to-letter morphism used in defining G_1 and obtain, thus, a derivation of the same form as (7.5) also according to G. Since this result is impossible, we conclude that no interpretation of G is self-embedding. Since every non-self-embedding grammar generates a regular language (this fact is easy to verify), we conclude that $\mathcal{L}(G)$ consists of only regular languages. $\square$

Lemma 7.5.   A grammar G is regular-sufficient if and only if, for some terminal letter a, the language a^+ is contained in $L(G)$. The latter condition is satisfied if and only if G possesses an a-restriction G_a such that $L(G_a) = a^+$.

Proof. The second sentence is obvious. It is also an immediate consequence of Lemma 7.2 that if no such terminal letter a is in G, then no language of the form b^+, where b is a letter, is in $\mathfrak{L}(G)$ and, hence, G is not regular-sufficient.

Assume that G possesses an a-restriction G_a such that $L(G_a) = a^+$. Consider an arbitrary regular language $R \subseteq \Sigma^+$. We shall prove that R is in $\mathfrak{L}(G_a)$. Consequently, R is also in $\mathfrak{L}(G)$, which shows that G is regular-sufficient.

To construct an interpretation G_1 of G_a generating our given language R, we use the standard triple construction. (Cf. Exercise 2.11.) The nonterminals of G_1 are triples (q, A, q'), where A is a nonterminal of G_a, and q and q' are nodes in the finite deterministic automaton representing R. Such a triple is an interpretation of A, i.e., belongs to the set $\sigma(A)$. The start symbols of G_1 are triples (q_0, S, q_F), where q_0 (resp. q_F) is the initial (resp. a final) node in the automaton, and S is a start symbol of G_a. The set of terminals of G_1 equals Σ, i.e., each letter of Σ is in $\sigma(a)$.

Let P_a be the production set of G_a. The production set of G_1 is the subset of $\sigma(P_a)$ which preserves both the derivations according to G_a and the transitions of the automaton. For instance, if

$$A \rightarrow BaCC$$

is a production of G_a, then the production set of G_1 contains all productions

$$(q_1, A, q_2) \rightarrow (q_1, B, q_3) \, b \, (q_4, C, q_5)(q_5, C, q_2),$$

where the q's are nodes of the automaton, and b is a letter of Σ causing a transition from q_3 to q_4. If $A \rightarrow ab$ is a production of G_a, then the production set of G_1 contains all productions

$$(q_1, A, q_2) \rightarrow ab,$$

where the q's are nodes of the automaton such that the word ab causes a transition from q_1 to q_2.

It should now be easy for the reader to define formally the production set of G_1 and to show that $L(G_1) = R$. $\square$

The following Theorem is an immediate corollary of Lemmas 7.4 and 7.5. The only additional fact needed is the decidability of the property of a grammar being self-embedding. This is quite straightforward; the details are left to the reader.

Theorem 7.6.   A grammar G is regular-complete if and only if G is not self-embedding and possesses an a-restriction G_a with the property $L(G_a) = a^+$. The regular-completeness of a grammar G is decidable.

Theorem 7.6 shows also that the family $\mathcal{L}$ of regular languages possesses the following property. Whenever a grammar G satisfies $\mathcal{L}(G) = \mathcal{L}$ then G possesses also an a-restriction G_a satisfying $\mathcal{L}(G_a) = \mathcal{L}$. Thus, only one terminal letter of G is "essential." Cf. also Exercise 7.

7.2   A DENSE HIERARCHY OF GRAMMATICAL FAMILIES

The main interest among grammatical families lies in certain widely studied ones, such as the families of regular, linear, or context-free languages. However, there are altogether "very many" grammatical families, because of the remarkable generative capacity of morphisms. To prove this proposition formally, we begin with some definitions.

Assume that $\mathcal{L}$ and $\mathcal{L}'$ are grammatical families such that $\mathcal{L} \subsetneqq \mathcal{L}'$. The pair $(\mathcal{L}, \mathcal{L}')$ is *dense* if, whenever, $\mathcal{L}_1$ and $\mathcal{L}_2$ are grammatical families satisfying

$$\mathcal{L} \subseteq \mathcal{L}_1 \subsetneqq \mathcal{L}_2 \subseteq \mathcal{L}',$$

then there is a grammatical family $\mathcal{L}_3$ such that $\mathcal{L}_1 \subsetneqq \mathcal{L}_3 \subsetneqq \mathcal{L}_2$. (The reader is warned against viewing the families between $\mathcal{L}$ and $\mathcal{L}'$ as linearly ordered; in general, there are many incomparable ones.)

A grammatical family $\mathcal{L}_2$ is a *successor* of a grammatical family $\mathcal{L}_1$ (and $\mathcal{L}_1$ is a *predecessor* of $\mathcal{L}_2$) if $\mathcal{L}_1 \subsetneqq \mathcal{L}_2$ and there is no grammatical family $\mathcal{L}_3$ with the property $\mathcal{L}_1 \subsetneqq \mathcal{L}_3 \subsetneqq \mathcal{L}_2$.

As an example, consider a grammar G and an integer $k \geq 1$ not belonging to the length set of $L(G)$. (For the definition of the length set, see Exercise 6.4.) Let $b_1, \ldots, b_k$ be new distinct terminal letters and let G_1 be the grammar obtained from G by adding the production

$$S \to b_1 \cdots b_k.$$

(As usual, S is a start letter.) Then it is easy to verify that $\mathcal{L}(G_1)$ is a successor of $\mathcal{L}(G)$. Here it is quite essential that the b's are distinct among themselves and also distinct from the terminal letters of G. It is also assumed that S does not appear on the right side of any production.

For instance, if G is determined by the productions

$$S \rightarrow A, \; A \rightarrow a^2 A, \; A \rightarrow a^2,$$

then by repeating the above construction we obtain an infinite sequence of grammatical families where each family is a successor (in the sense of the definition above) of the preceding one and where $\mathcal{L}(G)$ is the first family.

Hence, whenever the length set of $L(G')$ contains properly that of $L(G)$, then the pair $(\mathcal{L}(G), \mathcal{L}(G'))$ cannot be dense. On the other hand, many dense pairs are known where the length sets corresponding to the underlying grammars are the same. Our aim is to show that the families of regular and context-free languages constitute a dense pair.

Our next lemma is the essential tool in the proof. Before stating the lemma, we still define a useful auxiliary notion. A language L is *coherent* if it cannot be represented in the form $L = L_1 \cup L_2$, where L_1 and L_2 are languages over disjoint alphabets, and both L_1 and L_2 contain at least one nonempty word. Thus, the language $\{ab, bc, dc\}$ is coherent, whereas the language $\{a, bc\}$ is not.

Lemma 7.7. Assume that $\mathcal{L}_1$ and $\mathcal{L}_2$ are grammatical families such that $\mathcal{L}_1 \subsetneqq \mathcal{L}_2$ and, furthermore, that there is an infinite coherent language L in the difference $\mathcal{L}_2 \backslash \mathcal{L}_1$. Then there is a grammatical family $\mathcal{L}_3$ satisfying

$$\mathcal{L}_1 \subsetneqq \mathcal{L}_3 \subsetneqq \mathcal{L}_2. \tag{7.6}$$

Proof. For $i = 1, 2, \ldots$, denote by L_i the subset of L consisting of all words with length $\neq i$. We want to show that, for some number p, $L_p \notin \mathcal{L}_1$ and $L_p \neq L$.

Since L is infinite, there are infinitely many values of i with the property $L_i \neq L$. Assume that all such L_i are in $\mathcal{L}_1$. Let G_1 be the grammar generating $\mathcal{L}_1$, and H_i an interpretation of G_1 generating L_i. For each i, there is a letter-to-letter morphism h_i mapping H_i onto a subgrammar of G_1. Since the terminal alphabet of each H_i is contained in the alphabet of L, there are two distinct numbers i and j such that the restrictions of h_i and h_j to terminals are identical. (This follows because, clearly, there are only a finite number of letter-to-letter morphisms $h : \Sigma^* \rightarrow \Delta^*$, for any alphabets Σ and Δ.)

Consider now the languages L_i and L_j. Without loss of generality, we assume that the nonterminal alphabets of the grammars H_i and H_j are disjoint. Defining the union of morphisms, as well as the union of grammars in the natural way, we see that the union h of the morphisms h_i and h_j satisfies

$$H_i \cup H_j \in h^{-1}(G_1).$$

(For this conclusion, it is essential that h_i and h_j map terminals in the same way.) But this result means that the language $L_i \cup L_j = L$ is in $\mathcal{L}_1$, which contradicts our hypothesis.

Hence, there is a number p with the properties $L_p \notin \mathcal{L}_1$ and $L_p \neq L$. Clearly, any renaming of the nonterminal and terminal alphabets of a grammar leaves the language family of the grammar invariant. If necessary we rename the alphabets of G_1 and assume from now on that G_1 and H_p (the grammar for L_p) have no letters in common.

Consider the union G_3 of the grammars G_1 and H_p. (Thus, in G_3 each item is the union of the corresponding items in G_1 and H_p.) Denote

$$\mathcal{L}_3 = \mathcal{L}(G_3).$$

We claim that (7.6) holds.

By the definition of G_3, $\mathcal{L}_3$ contains $\mathcal{L}_1$. The containment is proper because L_p is not in $\mathcal{L}_1$ but, clearly, L_p is in $\mathcal{L}_3$.

Since L is in $\mathcal{L}_2$, also L_p is in $\mathcal{L}_2$. (This is a consequence of Exercise 6. It can also be verified directly by modifying the grammar for L in such a way that all words of length $\leq p$ are obtained directly from a start symbol. Cf. also the second sentence of Lemma 7.3.) Hence, we may assume that H_p is an interpretation of the grammar G_2 generating $\mathcal{L}_2$. By the last sentence of Lemma 7.1, $\mathcal{L}(H_p)$ is contained in $\mathcal{L}_2$.

Observe now that every language in $\mathcal{L}_3$ is of the form $K_1 \cup K_2$, where K_1 is in $\mathcal{L}_1$ and K_2 is in $\mathcal{L}(H_p)$ and, furthermore, that the alphabets of K_1 and K_2 are disjoint. The fact that $\mathcal{L}(H_p)$ and $\mathcal{L}_1$ are both contained in $\mathcal{L}_2$ implies that $\mathcal{L}_3$ is contained in $\mathcal{L}_2$. (Here the disjointness of the alphabets is quite essential; the conclusion is not necessarily valid otherwise.)

We now use the fact that the language L is coherent. This fact implies that if L is in $\mathcal{L}_3$, it must be in one of the parts of $\mathcal{L}_3$, i.e., either in $\mathcal{L}_1$ or in $\mathcal{L}(H_p)$. The first alternative is excluded by our hypothesis and the second alternative by the fact (see Lemma 7.2) that no language in $\mathcal{L}(H_p)$ contains words of length p. Because $L_p \neq L$, the language L contains at least one word of length p.

Consequently, the language L is in the difference $\mathcal{L}_2 \setminus \mathcal{L}_3$, which completes the verification of (7.6). $\square$

Theorem 7.8. The grammatical families of regular and context-free languages constitute a dense pair.

Proof. Consider two arbitrary grammatical families $\mathcal{L}_1$ and $\mathcal{L}_2$, $\mathcal{L}_1 \subsetneq \mathcal{L}_2$, lying between the families of regular and context-free languages. Thus, there is a language L in the difference $\mathcal{L}_2 \setminus \mathcal{L}_1$. Since $\mathcal{L}_1$ contains all regular and, hence, all finite languages, we conclude that L is infinite. In order to be able to apply Lemma 7.7, we still have to show that L is coherent. Of course, this need not be the case of the particular L we selected from the difference. However, we show that L possesses an infinite coherent subset L' lying in the difference $\mathcal{L}_2 \setminus \mathcal{L}_1$.

Thus, assume L is not coherent: $L = L_1 \cup L_2$, where L_1 and L_2 are languages over disjoint alphabets (and both L_1 and L_2 contain at least one nonempty word). Both L_1 and L_2 are in $\mathcal{L}_2$ because L is in $\mathcal{L}_2$. (This conclusion follows again either by Exercise 6 or by a direct argument concerning the grammar for L.) If both L_1 and L_2 were in $\mathcal{L}_1$, also L would be in $\mathcal{L}_1$, which is impossible. Thus, one of them, say L_1, is not in $\mathcal{L}_1$. The implication follows that L_1 is infinite (because $\mathcal{L}_1$ contains all finite languages).

We have, thus, found an infinite language L_1 belonging to the difference $\mathcal{L}_2 \setminus \mathcal{L}_1$. Furthermore, L_1 is over a smaller alphabet than L. If L_1 is not coherent, the same procedure is repeated. After finitely many steps, we find an infinite coherent language L' belonging to the difference $\mathcal{L}_2 \setminus \mathcal{L}_1$. Lemma 7.7 now applies. □

The effectiveness of the construction above is discussed in Exercise 8.

7.3 COLORINGS AND FAMILIES OF GRAPHS

We shall now apply the ideas presented in this chapter to the theory of graphs. This approach, introduced very recently, seems to be of special interest because of two reasons. In the first place, a classification of graphs is obtained, based on a notion that generalizes the notion of coloring in a natural way. In the second place, questions concerning this classification can be identified with questions concerning a fragment of the theory of grammar forms. Thus, we also exhibit an interesting link between language and graph theory.

In addition to digraphs introduced in Chapter 2, we shall consider also *undirected* graphs, referred to briefly as graphs. By definition, a *graph* is a pair (V, E), where V is a finite set whose elements are called *nodes* or *vertices* and E is a set of unordered pairs of elements of V. The elements of E are referred to as *lines* (in contrast to *arrows* in the case of digraphs). In what follows, it is assumed that the graphs and digraphs do not contain loops, i.e., lines or arrows from a vertex to itself. It is also assumed that each graph and digraph contains at least two vertices connected with a line or an arrow. We consider first unlabeled graphs and digraphs, and begin with the basic definitions.

A graph G' is an *interpretation* of a graph G if there is a mapping φ of the set of vertices of G' into the set of vertices of G such that, whenever there is a line between x and y in G', then there is also a line between $\varphi(x)$ and $\varphi(y)$ in G.

A digraph G' is an *interpretation* of a digraph G if there is a mapping φ of the set of vertices of G' into the set of vertices of G such that, whenever there is an arrow from x to y in G', then there is also an arrow from $\varphi(x)$ to $\varphi(y)$ in G.

Every graph (resp. digraph) G defines a family $\mathfrak{M}(G)$ of graphs (resp. digraphs), consisting of all interpretations of G. (Observe that we use the $\mathfrak{M}$-notation for the family of devices, "machines" or "models." The same notation was introduced for grammars. When we speak of the languages generated by the devices, we use the $\mathcal{L}$-notation.)

For two graphs G' and G, we say also that G' is *G-colorable* (or *colorable according to G*) if G' belongs to the family $\mathfrak{M}(G)$. A family of graphs is a *color-family* if it equals $\mathfrak{M}(G)$, for some graph G.

The motivation behind this terminology is the following. For $n \geq 2$, denote by K_n the complete graph with n vertices, i.e., the graph possessing an edge between every two distinct vertices. Clearly, a graph G is n-colorable in the usual graph-theoretic sense if and only if G belongs to $\mathfrak{M}(K_n)$. Thus, the Four-Color Theorem tells us that every planar graph is in $\mathfrak{M}(K_4)$!

On the other hand, in the customary theory of colorings only families $\mathfrak{M}(K_n)$ are considered. The definition above is much more general because colorings according to an arbitrary graph are considered.

For instance, consider the cyclic graph C_n with n vertices, i.e., the vertices are connected cyclically. The following illustration shows how C_7 is colored according to C_5.

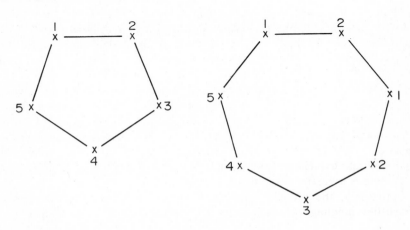

Thus C_7 is in $\mathfrak{M}(C_5)$. Intuitively, coloring according to C_5 means using the colors 1–5 in such a way that the adjacencies of C_5 are satisfied: if a vertex is colored by 1, then its neighbors may be colored by 2 or 5 but not by 3 or 4, and so forth. It is also easy to see that the reverse coloring is not possible: C_5 is not in $\mathfrak{M}(C_7)$.

Let us now discuss the language-theoretic meaning of the graph-theoretic notions introduced above. We identify a finite language F with the grammar G determined by the productions

$$S \to w, \quad w \in F.$$

Thus, we speak also of interpretations of F, as well as the family $\mathcal{L}(F)$ of languages generated by F. Clearly, a language L is in $\mathcal{L}(F)$ if and only if L is a subset of $\sigma(F)$, for some finite substitution σ such that $\sigma(a)$ is a finite set of letters for each letter a, and $a \neq b$ always implies $\sigma(a) \cap \sigma(b) = \phi$. Our identification of F and G is in accordance with Lemma 7.3, which shows that the language family of a finite grammar is completely determined by the language of the grammar.

The *reduced version* G_1 of a graph or digraph G is obtained from G by removing all isolated vertices, i.e., vertices not connected to any line or arrow. Clearly, $\mathfrak{M}(G_1) = \mathfrak{M}(G)$. (Recall our convention to the effect that all graphs and digraphs possess at least one line or arrow. Thus, by removing isolated vertices we never remove everything.)

A finite language is termed *graph-like* if it contains only words of length 2 and no words of the form a^2. To each graph-like language we may associate a digraph in the natural fashion: each letter denotes a vertex, and the words in the language indicate the arrows. For instance,

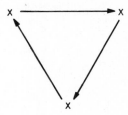

is the digraph associated to the language $\{ab, bc, ca\}$. The word ab indicates that there is an arrow from a to b.

Conversely, the reduced version of an arbitrary digraph determines a graph-like language which is unique up to the names of the letters. Thus, there is a one-to-one correspondence between graph-like languages and reduced digraphs.

The interconnection between graphs and languages, referred to above, is stated explicitly in the following lemma. The proof is omitted because it is immediate from the definitions.

Lemma 7.9.   Let F and F' be graph-like languages, and let G and G' be the corresponding digraphs. Then F' is an interpretation of F if and only if G' is an interpretation of G.

Lemma 7.9 expresses the fact that the following diagram commutes:

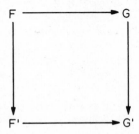

Thus, if we choose an interpretation F' of a (graph-like) language F and the digraph associated with F', the same effect is obtained by choosing an interpretation of the digraph G associated with F. The result shows also that all questions concerning hierarchies of digraph families can be reduced to questions concerning families determined by graph-like languages, and vice versa.

As regards graphs, the interconnection to language theory is analogous. The only difference is that one has to consider "commutative languages," i.e., the order of letters is immaterial. Thus, ab being in the language is equivalent to ba being in the language and means that the associated graph possesses a line between a and b. The notion of an interpretation can be defined for commutative languages as well. For instance, the commutative language

$$\{a_1a_2, a_2a_3, a_3a_4, a_4a_5, a_5a_6, a_6a_7, a_7a_1\}$$

is an interpretation of the commutative language

$$\{a_1a_2, a_2a_3, a_3a_4, a_4a_5, a_5a_1\},$$

which corresponds to the fact that the cyclic graph C_7 is an interpretation of C_5. In general the statement corresponding to Lemma 7.9 remains valid for graphs and commutative languages.

Lemma 7.9 and its counterpart for graphs show that results of Lemma 7.1 can be applied for digraphs and graphs. In particular, if G' is an interpretation of G (where G and G' are either graphs or digraphs) then $\mathfrak{M}(G')$ is contained in $\mathfrak{M}(G)$.

We now return to the discussion of color-families. Recall the definition of C_n and K_n, as well as the example of C_5 and C_7 given above. Along these lines, it is easy to establish the following doubly infinite hierarchy:

$$\cdots \mathfrak{M}(C_9) \subsetneqq \mathfrak{M}(C_7) \subsetneqq \mathfrak{M}(C_5) \subsetneqq \mathfrak{M}(C_3)$$
$$= \mathfrak{M}(K_3) \subsetneqq \mathfrak{M}(K_4) \subsetneqq \mathfrak{M}(K_5) \ldots . \qquad (7.7)$$

Clearly, for any n, $\mathfrak{M}(C_{2n}) = \mathfrak{M}(K_2)$. (This corresponds to the fact that a graph is 2-colorable if and only if it has no cycles of odd length.) Thus, it is essential that in (7.7) the cyclic graphs are of odd length.

The hierarchy (7.7) is a linear hierarchy of color-families. In general, the color-families are not ordered linearly. In fact, the following (strongest possible) incomparability result can be obtained.

Consider an arbitrary graph G. If all cycles in G are of even length, then $\mathfrak{M}(G) = \mathfrak{M}(K_2)$. This follows, for instance, by the criterion concerning 2-colorability. In fact, because we have assumed that all graphs considered possess at least one line, $\mathfrak{M}(K_2)$ is contained in every color-family.

Thus, assume G possesses a cycle of an odd length $2n + 1$. Since G is m-colorable, for some m, we obtain the inclusions

$$\mathfrak{M}(C_{2n+1}) \subseteq \mathfrak{M}(G) \subseteq \mathfrak{M}(K_m). \qquad (7.8)$$

Thus, every graph G satisfies either (7.8) or $\mathfrak{M}(G) = \mathfrak{M}(K_2)$. In particular, an arbitrary $\mathfrak{M}(G)$ can be incomparable with only finitely many $\mathfrak{M}(C_i)$ and finitely many $\mathfrak{M}(K_j)$ families. The following theorem shows that both numbers can be made arbitrarily large. The proof is omitted because graph theory beyond the scope of this book is required.

Theorem 7.10. For any integers $m \geq 3$ and $n \geq 2$, there is a graph G with the following properties.
(i) G is an interpretation of K_m but not of K_{m-1}.
(ii) C_{2n-1} is not an interpretation of G.

Consequently, each of the color-families

$$\mathfrak{M}(C_{2n-1}), \ldots, \mathfrak{M}(C_3) = \mathfrak{M}(K_3), \ldots, \mathfrak{M}(K_{m-1})$$

is incomparable with $\mathfrak{M}(G)$.

In analogy with grammatical families, we say that a color-family $\mathfrak{M}(G_2)$ is a *successor* of a color-family $\mathfrak{M}(G_1)$ if $\mathfrak{M}(G_1) \subsetneqq \mathfrak{M}(G_2)$ and there is no color-family $\mathfrak{M}(G_3)$ such that

$$\mathfrak{M}(G_1) \subsetneqq \mathfrak{M}(G_3) \subsetneqq \mathfrak{M}(G_2).$$

Recall that we have assumed that every graph possesses at least one line. If this assumption is not made, we consider the graph K_1 with only one vertex and no lines. It can be immediately verified that $\mathfrak{M}(K_2)$ is a successor of $\mathfrak{M}(K_1)$.

This trivial example is the only possible one about a successor, i.e., the color-families lie dense. This is further exploited in Exercises 9 and 13. Regarding digraph families, examples of successors are given in Exercise 10.

Finally, we want to indicate how similar ideas are applicable in a more general set-up. For instance, we might consider labeled graphs and, in particular, finite (nondeterministic) automata introduced in Chapter 2. Let us assume, further, that each automaton possesses exactly one initial node q_1 and exactly one final node q_2, $q_1 \neq q_2$, and that there is no arrow to q_1 and no arrow from q_2. It is left to the reader to verify that every λ-free regular language is represented by such an automaton.

Given two such automata G' and G, we say that G' is an interpretation of G if there is a mapping φ of the set of nodes of G' into the set of nodes of G, and a mapping ψ of the set of arrow labels of G' into the set of arrow labels of G such that, whenever there is an arrow labeled by a from x to y in G', then there is also an arrow labeled by $\psi(a)$ from $\varphi(x)$ to $\varphi(y)$ in G and, furthermore,

$$\varphi(q_1) = q_1, \varphi(q_2) = q_2,$$

and no other nodes are mapped by φ to q_1 or q_2. This definition is an extension of the one given above: it is also required that arrow labels, as well as initial and final nodes, are preserved.

On the other hand, a finite language F consisting of words of the form qaq' can be associated with such an automaton G. (The word qaq' indicates that there is in G an arrow labeled by a from q to q'. We assume that G has no isolated nodes.) Given two such finite languages F and F', we say that F' is an interpretation of F if (i) F' is a subset of $\sigma(F)$, where σ is a finite substitution as above, and (ii) $\sigma(q_1) = \{q_1\}$, $\sigma(q_2) = \{q_2\}$, and q_1 and q_2 do not appear otherwise in the range of σ.

It is now easy to verify that again the following diagram commutes:

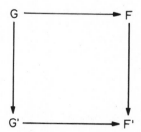

We can write the diagram also, as before, starting from F.

Denote by $\mathcal{L}(G)$ the family of languages represented by interpretations of G. It should be emphasized that the families $\mathcal{L}(F)$ are not any more in one-to-one correspondence with the families $\mathcal{L}(G)$. We may have $\mathcal{L}(G_1) = \mathcal{L}(G_2)$ although $\mathcal{L}(F_1)$ and $\mathcal{L}(F_2)$ are incomparable.

EXERCISES

1. A family $\mathcal{L}$ of languages is termed a *full AFL* if $\mathcal{L}$ is closed under each of the following operations: union, *, morphism, inverse morphism, and intersection with regular languages. Prove that every full AFL is closed under catenation and finite substitution.

2. Prove that the families of regular, context-free, and recursively enumerable languages constitute each a full AFL. (Our convention of restricting attention to λ-free languages is not applied here.) Prove, however, that the families of DOL and OL languages constitute both an "anti-AFL," i.e., are not closed under any of the AFL-operations. (For a comprehensive exposition on AFL theory, the reader is referred to [G2].)

3. Explain why in (7.2) we have G_1' instead of G_1. (For instance, consider the grammar H_1 determined by the production $S \rightarrow ab$, the grammar H_2 determined by the productions $S \rightarrow ab$, $S \rightarrow cd$, and the grammar H_3 determined by the productions $S \rightarrow ab$, $S \rightarrow ba$. What is the conclusion if you use G_1 in (7.2)? Does Lemma 7.3 remain valid?)

4. Formulate and prove the result corresponding to Theorem 7.6 for the family of all regular languages (instead of the λ-free ones considered in the text).

5. Consider the family of linear languages, i.e., languages generated by linear grammars. Develop a theory for linear-sufficiency and linear-completeness, corresponding to Lemma 7.5 and Theorem 7.6. This theory is considerably more complicated than the theory for regular languages. The reader may wish to consult [MSW 2].

6. Generalize the argument used in the proof of Lemma 7.5 to show that every grammatical family is closed under intersection with regular languages. In other words, if L is a language in the family and R is regular, then $L \cap R$ is in the family. Show also that the language family generated by a grammar with only one terminal letter is closed under union. Why is the assumption about one terminal needed?

7. A grammatical family $\mathcal{L}$ is termed *unary-complete* if, whenever a grammar G satisfies $\mathcal{L}(G) = \mathcal{L}$, then G also possesses an a-restriction G_a satisfying $\mathcal{L}(G_a) = \mathcal{L}$. Study the notion of unary-completeness. (Theorem 7.6 shows that the family of regular languages is unary-complete. The same holds true for linear languages, cf. Exercise 5. It can also be shown that the family of context-free languages is unary-complete.)

8. Show that the construction in the proof of Theorem 7.8 is effective in the following sense. Assume that it is known that $\mathcal{L}_1 \subsetneqq \mathcal{L}_2$ and that a language L in the difference $\mathcal{L}_2 \backslash \mathcal{L}_1$ is given. Then one can construct effectively a grammatical family $\mathcal{L}_3$ satisfying $\mathcal{L}_1 \subsetneqq \mathcal{L}_3 \subsetneqq \mathcal{L}_2$. (The problem of deciding the equivalence between two grammatical families, i.e., whether or not $\mathcal{L}(G_1) = \mathcal{L}(G_2)$ holds for arbitrary two given context-free grammars G_1 and G_2, is open.)

9. Show that there is a color-family between any two families in the hierarchy (7.7). (Consider an odd number of cycles "glued" together.)

10. Show that the digraph family associated with the language $L_2 = \{ab, bc\}$ is a successor of the digraph family associated with the language $\{ab\}$. (The notion of a successor is defined in exactly the same way as for color-families.) Show, however, that the digraph family associated with the language $L_3 = \{ab, bc, cd\}$ is not a successor of the digraph family associated with L_2. Show that the digraph family associated with the language $\{ab, bc_1, b_1c_1, b_1c, cd\}$ is a predecessor of that associated with L_3. (Cf. [MSW 4] for a discussion of the hierarchies involved. No examples of successors are known if the digraphs are more complicated, for instance, if they contain cycles.)

11. Observe that every graph (resp. digraph) is an interpretation of a graph (resp. digraph) containing a loop. This is the basic reason why such graphs and digraphs were excluded from our discussion. Show that the digraph family associated with the language $\{a^2\}$ possesses no predecessor.

12. Associate a finite language with each context-free grammar. Consider interpretations of such languages, as well as interpretations of original grammars.

Establish a commuting diagram, and also discuss its relevance to the family of languages generated by all interpretations of a grammar.

13. Show that the color-families lie dense, i.e., that there is a color-family strictly between any two color-families, one of which is strictly contained in the other. *Hints.* Consider first an arbitrary cyclic graph of the form C_{2m+1}. Show that there are arbitrarily large connected graphs H such that (i) H is an interpretation of C_{2m+1} but not vice versa, and (ii) if any two non-adjacent nodes in H are identified then C_{2m+1} is an interpretation of the resulting graph. Conclude that there is no graph having C_{2m+1} as a successor. Extend this conclusion to an arbitrary connected graph G, where C_{2m+1} appears as the smallest odd cycle, by "replacing" one occurrence of this cycle with H. Finally, the extension to non-connected graphs will be easy. (This exercise is based on the work of E. Welzl, personal communication.)

HISTORICAL AND
BIBLIOGRAPHICAL REMARKS

The main purpose of the subsequent remarks is to point out some general lines of development, as well as to give hints to the interested reader concerning specific details and material related to the text. We do not try to credit each individual result to some specific author(s), which would be rather difficult in some cases.

The material in Chapter 1 originates from [T 1] and [T 2]. The exposition is entirely different, though, and also uses some ideas from [MoH 2], Lemma 1.10 being from [EhR 4].

There is a huge literature concerning matters related to Chapter 2. For material concerning finite automata and regular expressions, the reader is referred to [Sa 1] and [McP]. For formal languages and the Chomsky hierarchy, each of the references [Har], [HU], [Mau], [Sa 2] is rather comprehensive. [AU] considers the theory from the point of view of parsing. [G 1] and [Be 3] both present a theory of context-free languages. [ChS], [GR], and [Niv] are some of the basic original references about context-free languages. The large and important area of complexity theory of formal languages is not at all discussed in this book; the reader is referred to [AHU], [HU] and [Bo]. [Kl] is the original reference to Kleene's Theorem, and [Ch] to grammars.

Theorem 3.2 is due to [DeS]; our exposition follows largely [Sa 1]. Two entirely different solutions to the FPP problem are given in [ManS] and [Has]; our exposition is based on ideas in the latter. The FPP problem is originally due to J. Brzozowski.

Most of the original results about codes are due to Schützenberger; [La] is a recent exposition containing much of the theory. For more information on maximal codes, [Mar] is an important reference. Equality sets and elementary morphisms were introduced in [EhR 1] and [EhR 2]. [P] is the original reference to the Post correspondence problem; detailed discussions are contained in [Har], [Mau], and [Sa 2].

The DOL sequence equivalence problem was first solved in [CuF]; our presentation follows the essentially simpler solution in [EhR 2] and [RS]. The proof of Lemma 5.7 is according to [Sa 3]; [RS] contains further references related to this matter.

[Niv] and especially [McP] are basic references for local and k-testable languages. Theorem 6.2 is from [CuM]. The original version of Lemma 6.4 is from [Gr 1]. Theorem 6.5 is due to [Sh]; the version of Theorem 6.7 appears in [Gr 2]. For further discussion of representations in terms of equality sets, the reader is referred to [BoB], [Cu], [CuM], [EnR], [RS], and [Sa 5]. Theorem 6.11 is originally due to [St].

[CrG] is the first paper on grammar forms; however, it has a different notion for interpreting terminals, which makes morphic considerations impossible. The material in the three sections of Chapter 7 is from [MSW 2], [MSW 3], and [MSW 4], respectively.

The subsequent list of references contains only works referred to in this book. It is by no means intended to be a bibliography on formal languages or a collection of the best papers in the area. Many of the books listed below contain extensive bibliographies.

REFERENCES

[AHU]   A. AHO, J. HOPCROFT, and J. ULLMAN. *The Design and Analysis of Computer Algorithms.* Addison-Wesley, Reading (1974).

[AU]   A. AHO and J. ULLMAN. *The Theory of Parsing, Translation and Compiling, I-II.* Prentice-Hall, Englewood Cliffs (1972-1973).

[Be 1]   J. BERSTEL. "Sur les mots sans carré définis par un morphisme." *Springer Lecture Notes in Computer Science 71* (1979) 16-25.

[Be 2]   J. BERSTEL. "Mots sans carré et morphismes itérés." Université Paris 7, Institut de Programmation, 78-42 (1978).

[Be 3]   J. BERSTEL. *Transductions and Context-Free Languages.* B. G. Teubner, Stuttgart (1979).

[Bo]   R. BOOK. "Formal language theory and theoretical computer science." *Springer Lecture Notes in Computer Science 33* (1975) 1-15.

[BoB]   R. BOOK and F.-J. BRANDENBURG. "Representing complexity classes by equality sets." *Springer Lecture Notes in Computer Science 71* (1979) 49-57.

[Ch]   N. CHOMSKY. "Three models for the description of language." *IRE Transactions on Information Theory IT-2* (1956) 113-124.

[ChS]   N. CHOMSKY and M. P. SCHÜTZENBERGER. "The algebraic theory of context-free languages." In P. BRAFFORT and D. HIRSCHBERG (eds.), *Computer Programming and Formal Systems.* North Holland Publ., Amsterdam (1963) 118-161.

[CrG]   A. CREMERS and S. GINSBURG. "Context-free grammar forms." *Journal of Computer and System Sciences 11* (1975) 86-116.

[Cu]   K. CULIK II. "A purely homomorphic characterization of recursively enumerable sets." *Journal of the Association for Computing Machinery 26* (1979) 345-350.

[CuF]   K. CULIK II and I. FRIS. "The decidability of the equivalence problem for DOL-systems." *Information and Control 35* (1977) 20-39.

[CuK]   K. CULIK II and J. KARHUMÄKI. "On the equality sets for homomorphisms on free monoids with two generators." *R.A.I.R.O. Informatique théorique 14* (1980), to appear.

[CuM]   K. CULIK II and H. MAURER. "On simple representations of language families." *R.A.I.R.O. Informatique théorique 13* (1979) 241-250.

[CuS]   K. CULIK II and A. SALOMAA. "On the decidability of homomorphism equivalence for languages." *Journal of Computer and System Sciences 17* (1978) 163-175.

[De]   F. DEJEAN. "Sur un théorême de Thue." *Journal of Combinatorial Theory* (A) 13 (1972) 90-99.

[DeS]   F. DEJEAN and M. P. SCHÜTZENBERGER. "On a question of Eggan." *Information and Control 9* (1966) 23-25.

[EhR 1]   A. EHRENFEUCHT and G. ROZENBERG. "Simplifications of homomorphisms." *Information and Control 38* (1978) 298–309.

[EhR 2]   A. EHRENFEUCHT and G. ROZENBERG. "Elementary homomorphisms and a solution of the DOL sequence equivalence problem." *Theoretical Computer Science 7* (1978) 169–183.

[EhR 3]   A. EHRENFEUCHT and G. ROZENBERG. "On a bound for the DOL sequence equivalence problem." *Theoretical Computer Science 12* (1980) 339–342.

[EhR 4]   A. EHRENFEUCHT and G. ROZENBERG. "On the subword complexity of square-free DOL languages." *Theoretical Computer Science,* to appear.

[Ei]   S. EILENBERG. *Automata, Languages and Machines, Vol. A.* Academic Press, New York (1974).

[EnR]   J. ENGELFRIET and G. ROZENBERG. "Fixed point languages, equality languages and representation of recursively enumerable languages." *Journal of the Association for Computing Machinery 27* (1980) 499–518.

[G 1]   S. GINSBURG. *The Mathematical Theory of Context-Free Languages.* McGraw-Hill, New York (1966).

[G 2]   S. GINSBURG. *Algebraic and Automata-Theoretic Properties of Formal Languages.* North Holland Publ., Amsterdam (1975).

[GR]   S. GINSBURG and H. RICE. "Two families of languages related to ALGOL." *Journal of the Association for Computing Machinery 9* (1962) 350–371.

[Gr 1]   S. GREIBACH. "A new normal form theorem for context-free phrase structure grammars." *Journal of the Association for Computing Machinery 12* (1965) 42–52.

[Gr 2]   S. GREIBACH. "The hardest context-free language." *S.I.A.M. Journal of Computing 2* (1973) 304–310.

[H]   M. HALL, Jr. "Generators and relations in groups—the Burnside problem." In T. L. SAATY (ed.), *Lectures on Modern Mathematics, Vol. II,* 42–92. John Wiley and Sons, New York (1964).

[Har]   M. HARRISON. *Introduction to Formal Language Theory.* Addison-Wesley, Reading (1978).

[Has]   K. HASHIGUCHI. "A decision procedure for the order of regular events." *Theoretical Computer Science 8* (1979) 69–72.

[HU]   J. HOPCROFT and J. ULLMAN. *Introduction to Automata Theory, Languages and Computation.* Addison-Wesley, Reading (1979).

[KaS]   J. KARHUMÄKI and I. SIMON. "A note on elementary homomorphisms and the regularity of equality sets." *E.A.T.C.S. Bulletin 9* (1979) 16–24.

[Kl]   S. C. KLEENE. "Representation of events in nerve nets and finite automata." In *Automata Studies,* Princeton Univ. Press, Princeton (1956).

[La]   G. LALLEMENT. *Semigroups and Combinatorial Applications.* John Wiley and Sons, New York (1979).

[Le]   Y. LECERF. "Récursive insolubilité de l'équation générale de diagona-
         lisation de deux monomorphismes de monoides libres $\phi x = \psi x$." *C. R.
         Acad. Sci. Paris 257* (1963) 2940-2943.

[L]   A. LINDENMAYER. "Mathematical models for cellular interaction in
         development I-II." *Journal of Theoretical Biology 18* (1968) 280-315.

[Li 1]   M. LINNA. "Finite power property of regular languages." In M. NIVAT
         (ed.), *Automata, Languages and Programming,* North Holland Publ.,
         Amsterdam (1973) 87-98.

[Li 2]   M. LINNA. "The DOL-ness for context-free languages is decidable." *In-
         formation Processing Letters 5* (1976) 149-151.

[Li 3]   M. LINNA. "The decidability of the DOL prefix problem." *International
         Journal of Computer Mathematics 6* (1977) 127-142.

[LyS]   R. LYNDON and M. P. SCHÜTZENBERGER. "The equation $a^M =
         b^N c^P$ in a free group." *Michigan Mathematical Journal 9* (1962) 289-298.

[ManS]   A. MANDEL and I. SIMON. "On finite semigroups of matrices."
         Theoretical Computer Science 5 (1978) 101-111.

[Mar]   A. A. MARKOV. "Uslovija polnoty dlja neraznomernykh kodov." *Prob-
         lemy Kibernetiki 9* (1963) 327-331.

[Mau]   H. MAURER. *Theoretische Grundlagen der Programmiersprachen.*
         Bibliographisches Institut, Mannheim (1969).

[MSW 1] H. MAURER, A. SALOMAA and D. WOOD. "On generators and
         generative capacity of EOL forms." *Acta Informatica 13* (1980) 87-107.

[MSW 2] H. MAURER, A. SALOMAA and D. WOOD. "Context-free grammar
         forms with strict interpretations." *Journal of Computer and System
         Sciences 21* (1980) 110-135.

[MSW 3] H. MAURER, A. SALOMAA and D. WOOD. "Dense hierarchies of
         grammatical families." *Journal of the Association for Computing
         Machinery,* to appear.

[MSW 4] H. MAURER, A. SALOMAA and D. WOOD. "Colorings and interpreta-
         tions: a connection between graphs and grammar forms." *Discrete
         Mathematics,* to appear.

[Mc]   D. McLEAN. "Idempotent semigroups." *American Mathematical
         Monthly 61* (1954) 110-113.

[McP]   R. McNAUGHTON and S. PAPERT. *Counter-Free Automata.* M.I.T.
         Press, Cambridge (1971).

[MiS]   M. MORISAKI and K. SAKAI. "A complete axiom system for rational
         sets with multiplicity." *Theoretical Computer Science 11* (1980) 79-92.

[MoH 1] M. MORSE and G. HEDLUND. "Symbolic dynamics." *American Jour-
         nal of Mathematics 60* (1938) 815-866.

[MoH 2] M. MORSE and G. HEDLUND. "Unending chess, symbolic dynamics,
         and a problem in semigroups." *Duke Mathematical Journal 11* (1944) 1-7.

[Nie]   M. NIELSEN. "On the decidability of some equivalence problems for
         DOL systems." *Information and Control 25* (1974) 166-193.

[Niv]   M. NIVAT. "Transductions des langages de Chomsky." *Ann. Inst.
         Fourier, Grenoble 18* (1968) 339-456.

[P]   E. POST. "A variant of a recursively unsolvable problem." *Bulletin of the American Mathematical Society 52* (1946) 264-268.

[RS]   G. ROZENBERG and A. SALOMAA. *The Mathematical Theory of L Systems.* Academic Press, New York (1980).

[Ru 1]   K. RUOHONEN. "The decidability of the FOL-DOL equivalence problem." *Information Processing Letters 8* (1979) 257-260.

[Ru 2]   K. RUOHONEN. "The inclusion problem for DOL languages." *Elektronische Informationsverarbeitung und Kybernetik 15* (1980) 535-548.

[Sa 1]   A. SALOMAA. *Theory of Automata.* Pergamon Press, Oxford (1969).

[Sa 2]   A. SALOMAA. *Formal Languages.* Academic Press, New York (1973).

[Sa 3]   A. SALOMAA. "On sentential forms of context-free grammars." *Acta Informatica 2* (1973) 40-49.

[Sa 4]   A. SALOMAA. "Comparative decision problems between sequential and parallel rewriting." *Proc. Symp. Uniformly Structured Automata and Logic.* Tokyo (1975) 62-66.

[Sa 5]   A. SALOMAA. "Equality sets for homomorphisms of free monoids." *Acta Cybernetica 4* (1978) 127-139.

[Sal S]   A. SALOMAA and M. SOITTOLA. *Automata-Theoretic Aspects of Formal Power Series.* Springer-Verlag, Berlin (1978).

[SarP]   A. SARDINAS and C. PATTERSON. "A necessary and sufficient condition for the unique decomposition of coded messages." *IRE Intern. Conv. Record 8* (1953) 104-108.

[Sh]   E. SHAMIR. "A representation theorem for algebraic and context-free power series in noncommuting variables." *Information and Control 11* (1967) 239-254.

[St]   D. STANAT. "A homomorphism theorem for weighted context-free grammars." *Journal of Computer and System Sciences 6* (1972) 217-232.

[T 1]   A. THUE. "Über unendliche Zeichenreihen." *Videnskapsselskapets Skrifter.* I. Mat.-naturv. Klasse, Kristiania (1906) 1-22.

[T 2]   A. THUE. "Über die gegenseitige Lage gleicher Teile gewisser Zeichenreihen." *Videnskapsselskapets Skrifter.* I. Mat.-naturv. Klasse, Kristiania (1912) 1-67.

[W]   D. WOOD. *Grammar and L Forms: An Introduction.* Springer-Verlag, Berlin (1980).

INDEX

143